GARLAND STUDIES IN

AMERICAN POPULAR HISTORY AND CULTURE

edited by

JEROME NADELHAFT
UNIVERSITY OF MAINE

A GARLAND SERIES

Garland Studies in American Popular History and Culture

Jerome Nadelhaft, series editor

Seduction, Prostitution, and
Moral Reform in New York,
1830–1860
Larry Whiteaker

Hollywood's Vision of Team
Sports: Heroes, Race, and
Gender
Deborah V. Tudor

The Flamingo in the Garden:
American Yard Art and the
Vernacular Landscape
Colleen J. Sheehy

Textual Vehicles: The
Automobile in American
Literature
Roger N. Casey

Film and the Nuclear Age:
Representing Cultural Anxiety
Toni A. Perrine

Lesbian and Gay Memphis:
Building Communities Behind
the Magnolia Curtain
Daneel Buring

Making Villains, Making
Heroes: Joseph R. McCarthy,
Martin Luther King, Jr., and
the Politics of American
Memory
Gary Daynes

America Under Construction:
Boundaries and Identities in
Popular Culture
Kristi S. Long and Matthew
Nadelhaft, editors

AIDS, Social Change, and
Theater: Performance as
Protest
Cindy J. Kistenberg

African American Nationalist
Literature of the 1960s: Pens
of Fire
Sandra Hollin Flowers

The Rehabilitation of
Richard Nixon: The Media's
Effect on Collective Memory
Thomas J. Johnson

Chicano Images: Refiguring
Ethnicity in Mainstream Film
Christine List

At a Theater or Drive-in Near
You: The History, Culture,
and Politics of the American
Exploitation Film
Randall Clark

Lolita in Peyton Place:
Highbrow, Lowbrow, and
Middlebrow Novels of the
1950s
Ruth Wood

Contra Dance Choreography:
A Reflection of Social Change
Mary Dart

The Intellectual Origins of
Mass Parties and Mass Schools
in the Jacksonian Era: Creating a Conformed Citizenry
Julie M. Walsh

Understanding Elvis: Southern
Roots vs. Star Image
Susan M. Doll

Hollywood's Frontier
Captives: Cultural Anxiety
and the Captivity Plot in
American Film
Barbara Mortimer

Public Lives, Private Virtues:
Images of American
Revolutionary War Heroes,
1782–1832
Christopher Harris

The Lyrics of Civility: Biblical
Images and Popular Music
Lyrics in American Culture
Kenneth G. Bielen

PUBLIC LIVES, PRIVATE VIRTUES

IMAGES OF AMERICAN REVOLUTIONARY WAR HEROES, 1782–1832

CHRISTOPHER HARRIS

GARLAND PUBLISHING, INC.
A MEMBER OF THE TAYLOR & FRANCIS GROUP
NEW YORK & LONDON / 2000

Published in 2000 by
Garland Publishing Inc.
A Member of the Taylor & Francis Group
19 Union Square West
New York, NY 10003

10   9   8   7   6   5   4   3   2   1

Library of Congress Cataloging-in-Publication Data
Harris, Chistopher.
     Public lives, private virtues : images of American Revolutionary War
heroes, 1782–1832 / Christopher Harris.
          p. cm. — (Garland studies in American popular history and culture)
     Includes bibliographcal references and index.
     ISBN 0-8153-3482-6 (alk. paper)
          1. United States—History—Revolution, 1775–1783 Biography. 2. States-
men—United States Biography. 3. United States—History—Revolution,
1775–1783—Historiography. 4. Statesmen—United States—Historiography.
5. Washington, George, 1732–1799. 6. Weems, M.L. (Mason Locke), 1759–
1825. Life of George Washington. I. Title. II. Series.
E206.H27 1999
973.3'092'2—dc21   99-43611

Printed on acid-free, 250-year-life paper
Manufactured in the United States of America

071602—4840H6

To Christine

Contents

List of Illustrations   ix
Preface   xiii

1. Bright Examples: Biographies of Revolutionary Heroes   3
      Conventions of Eighteenth-Century Biography   6
      Mason Locke Weems and His Market   10
      Weems' Biography of George Washington   13
      Weems' Revision of 1808   19

2. "Domestick Subjects": Revolutionary Heroes in American
      Magazines   29
      George Washington   31
      Other Heroes   38

3. Forming Republican Citizens: Schoolbook Accounts of
      Revolutionary Heroes   45
      The Nature of School Readers in the Early Republic   47
      Weems' *Life of George Washington* as a Schoolbook   51
      Illustrations of Heroes   56
      Written Accounts of Heroes   61

4. Portraits of Virtue and the Advent of Realism   71
      Psychological Theories of Example   75
      Theories of Example in American Education   79
      The Portrayal of Affectionate Relationships   82
      The Persistence of Classical Republican Virtues   90
      The Advent of Realism   95

Notes   107
Illustrations   135
Index   167

List of Illustrations

1. George Washington, from
   The Columbian Magazine, 1788

2. George Washington, from
   The Massachusetts Magazine, 1791

3. George Washington Esqr., from
   The Philadelphia Monthly Magazine, or Universal Repository,
   1798

4. George Washington, from
   The Boston Magazine, 1784

5. Genl. Washington, from
   The Monthly Military Repository, 1796

6. George Washington, from
   The South Carolina Weekly Museum, 1797

7. General Washington's Resignation, from
   The Philadelphia Magazine and Review, 1799

8. Britannia, from
   George Richardson, *Iconology*, 1779

9. Patriotism, from
   George Richardson, *Iconology*, 1779

10. George Washington, from
    The New York Mirror, 1831

11. Major General Warren, from
    The Boston Magazine, 1784

12.   Maj^r. Genl. Greene, from
The Columbian Magazine, 1786

13.   Gen. Wayne, from
The Polyanthos, 1806

14.   Nicholas Biddle, from
The Port Folio, 1809

15.   Anthony Wayne, from
The Port Folio, 1809

16.   Daniel Morgan, from
The Port Folio, 1812

17.   Henry Knox, from
The Port Folio, 1811

18.   George Washington, from
Mason Locke Weems, *The Life and Memorable Actions of George Washington*, 1800.

19.   George Washington, from
Mason Locke Weems, *A History . . . of George Washington . . .*, 2nd ed.,1800

20.   George Washington, from
Mason Locke Weems, *A History . . . of George Washington . . .*, 3rd ed.,1800

21.   Death of Genl. Montgomery, from
Mason Locke Weems, *The Life of George Washington . . .*, 8th ed., 1809

22.   Battle of Bunker's Hill & Death of Gen. Warren, from
Mason Locke Weems, *The Life of George Washington . . .*, 8th ed., 1809

23.   Sisyphus, from
Geffery Whitney, *A Choice of Emblems*, 1586

24.   G. Washington, from
The New England Primer, Much Improved, 1796

25.   His Excellency Gen. Washington, President of the United States, from
The History of America, Abridged for the Use of Children, 1795

26.   Israel Putnam and the Wolf, from
Noah Webster, *Little Reader's Assistant*, 1790

27. Death of General Warren, from
    [Samuel Griswold Goodrich], *The First Book of History, for Children and Youth*, 1831

28. Israel Putnam and the Wolf, from
    Juvenile Miscellany, 1827

29. Oh my father! my father! I will die with you!!, from
    Mason Locke Weems, *The Life of Gen. Francis Marion*, 7th ed., 1821

30. Genl. Warren taking leave of his wife and child on the eve of the battle of Bunker Hill, from
    The Columbian Magazine, n.d.

Preface

Biographers, magazine editors, and schoolbook authors of the early republic believed that written and visual portraits of American Revolutionary heroes could stimulate readers to act virtuously. Sympathetic identification with the war's heroes, who exemplified classical republican virtues, would engender in Americans those virtues thought necessary for the continued good health of the nation. But the notion of what constitutes virtuous behavior was changing during the fifty years following the Revolution. Eighteenth-century classical virtues required putting aside self interest for the community's good. After the Revolution, Americans increasingly embraced self-interest, as suited a people increasingly concerned with economic growth, the accumulation of wealth, and the pursuit of social status.

The biographies, magazine articles, and schoolbooks examined in this book show little of this important change. There was near unanimous agreement among those who created portraits of the Revolution's war heroes that classical republican virtues matter, and matter deeply. Even bookseller and author Mason Locke Weems, whom historians have come to see as a prime example of emerging bourgeois values, promoted classical republican virtues. Although his colorful letters provide ample evidence of changing morality in America, his *Life of Washington* in its various versions sings the praises of the classical virtues—disinterested benevolence, equanimity, temperance, piety, sincerity, and industry. To write his *Life of Washington*, Weems used the prevailing form of biography, recounting Washington's public career and concluding with a list of the hero's virtues. Weems modified the form in 1808 by adding stories of

Washington's private life. In 1812 he attempted something more radical, writing *The Life of Gen. Francis Marion* as a historical romance. Although Weems fell short of his goal, he created a book with touches of realism not found in other early national biographies.

Apart from George Washington and Francis Marion, the "swamp fox," the heroes discussed in the pages that follow are likely to be unknown to most Americans. We have largely forgotten the writings of biographers, magazine writers, and schoolbook authors prominent during the years following the Revolution. Without the help of an emblem book, we can no longer read the visual language some illustrators used to create portraits of virtue, and the schoolbooks of the period are of interest primarily to historians and book collectors. Few Americans, however, would consider the concerns voiced in the biographies, magazines, and schoolbooks to be remote from their lives. Those who created portraits of Revolutionary heroes debated how private virtue influences public life, worried about declining standards of morality, and sought ways to teach values they believed to be crucial to the future of their children and the nation. The debate, worries, and efforts to teach values remain with us today.

Fifteen years have passed since I completed the first version of this book. At that time, I benefited greatly from the direction, support, and criticism of three scholars at Brown University. Barton St. Armand, who guided me through the vicissitudes of research and writing, was unwavering in his enthusiasm for this project. Gordon S. Wood provided keen advice about writing history. I have drawn extensively on his scholarship of the early republic to understand portraits of Revolutionary heroes. Thomas Adams, then Librarian of the John Carter Brown Library and now Librarian Emeritus, taught me the rewards of looking closely at a book's paper, type, and binding, as well as the content of its text. Occupied with other endeavors for two decades, I was able to take a fresh look at my work when I picked it up again last year. I have changed much of its form and argument without the guidance of the three men who initially helped me so much. What faults the reader may find in *Public Lives, Private Virtues* are solely my own.

For the original version, I spent the better part of two years in libraries examining biographies, magazines, and schoolbooks. I thank the staffs of Harvard University's Widener, Gutman, and Houghton libraries, who helped me along with this work. The Boston Athenaeum offered an idyllic place to write. Curators of prints at various libraries noted throughout the book were gracious in helping me locate portraits of Revolutionary heroes. I especially thank Laura Monti and Roberta Zongi of the Boston Public Library, Georgia B. Barnhill of the American Antiquarian Society, and Sally Pierce of the Boston Athenaeum.

I want to express my gratitude to the editors of *The Southern Literary Journal*, which published a version of chapter 1. I thank Jerome Nadelhaft, Garland's series editor, for deciding my dissertation showed enough promise to revise and publish. I am grateful also to Marjorie Manwaring for providing the last edit of the manuscript before it went to press, and to Elizabeth Eisenhood for her index.

And I thank my wife, Christine. Without her editorial talents, humor, and tolerance for my single-mindedness, I could not have written *Public Lives, Private Virtues*. I lovingly dedicate the book to her.

Christopher Harris

Public Lives, Private Virtues

Bright Examples: Biographies of Revolutionary Heroes

The first book-length biography praising the virtues and recounting the exploits of a Revolutionary hero appeared in 1788, five years after the Treaty of Paris formally ended the war. David Humphreys, aide-de-camp to Washington during the Revolution, and a Connecticut Wit, offered Americans his life of Israel Putnam, a Connecticut native like the author himself. Apart from *An Essay on the Life of the Honorable Major-General Israel Putnam*, which Humphreys completed during an extended stay at Mt. Vernon in 1787 and early 1788, the only other biography of a Revolutionary hero to be published before 1800 was *The Life of General Washington*. This too was a Humphreys work, part of a biography that he labored over, but eventually abandoned, during his time at Mt. Vernon. Attributed to Jedidiah Morse, the Humphrey piece first appeared in Morse's *American Geography* and was later reprinted in several memorials to Washington. Following Washington's death, biographies increased in number as the cult of Washington grew, creating a larger market for the books. Sensing the demand for a Washington biography, in 1800 Mason Locke Weems rushed to press his *Life and Memorable Actions of George Washington*. A year later Philadelphia printer Joseph Charless brought out the first American edition of Irish journalist John Corry's *Life of Washington*. Another Philadelphian, C. P. Wayne, published John Marshall's five-volume *Life of George Washington* between 1804 and 1808, while Aaron Bancroft's abridged version of the Marshall biography and David Ramsay's *Life of George Washington* appeared in 1807. Publishers brought to market book-length biographies of other Revolutionary heroes. Weems, seeking to profit from the success of his Washington biography, obtained from a friend of Francis Marion letters that Weems transformed into his highly original *Life of Gen. Francis Marion*. If not as popular as the Washington biography, the Marion book attracted enough buyers to merit numerous editions for several decades. The same success did not meet William Dobein James' own, conventional biography of Marion. Between 1819 and 1825 Charles Caldwell, a physician and editor of the *Port Folio*, and William Johnson, a South Carolinian jurist, wrote lives of Nathaniel Greene. John Henry Sherburne's biography of John Paul Jones also appeared during this time.[1]

In addition to full-length biographies, printers began to issue compilations of biographical materials and sketches. W. S. Baker's *Bibliotheca Washingtoniana* provides a reasonable measure of the interest in this type of book, which consisted of a collection of letters, speeches, and miscellaneous documents regarding a hero, and often a brief biographical sketch. Baker lists twenty-three occurrences of compilation books on Washington issued between 1782 and 1832. Among the collections published in 1800 in response to Washington's death were *Washington's Political Legacies*, which included a biographical sketch by John M. Williams, and Thomas Condie's *Biographical Memoirs of the Illustrious Gen. George Washington*. Condie's book reprinted, with several minor additions, letters and documents related to Washington, as well as a biographical sketch that had appeared three years earlier in the *Philadelphia Monthly Magazine*. William Allen's *An American Biographical and Historical Dictionary*, published in 1809, included biographical profiles of Major Andre, Horatio Gates, Nathaniel Greene, Henry Knox, Charles Lee, Francis Marion, Israel Putnam, Philip Schuyler, Joseph Warren, Washington, and Anthony Wayne. None were original. The Washington sketch, for example, was stitched together from the biographies of Marshall, Ramsey, and Bancroft. A year later John Kingston issued *The New American Biographical Dictionary*, which included much of the same material as Allen's dictionary. Kingston compiled sketches of Gates, Greene, Marion, Warren, Washington, and Wayne from previously published portraits in magazines and biographies. Between 1817 and 1819 three more biographical dictionaries were published. *Delaplaine's Repository of the Lives and Portraits of Distinguished Americans,* another Philadelphia product, is worth noting for its entry on Washington. Although the dictionary included a handsome portrait after Houdon, the writer of the biographical sketch concluded that the "pencil and the chisel have vied with each other in a laudable attempt to perpetuate [Washington's] likeness. But the project has failed . . . His likeness was concentered in himself alone, and those who have never beheld it there, will search for it in vain on canvass or in marble." The first volume of Thomas Wilson's two-volume *Biography of Principle Military and Naval Heroes Comprehending Details of Their Achievements during the Revolutionary and Late Wars* contained brief biographies of Revolutionary heroes. And Thomas Woodward offered biographical sketches of Greene, Warren, Washington, and Wayne in his *Columbian Plutarch.*[2]

Written in conventional eighteenth century style, most biographies and biographical sketches were essentially histories of the public careers of the heroes, with short recitations of character traits tagged on the end. William's sketch in *Washington's Political Legacies* was typical. After presenting Washington's lineage and public career in twenty-eight pages, Williams concluded that the hero had the "urbanity of a gentleman, without the littleness of pride; and in the very plenitude of his authority, would sheathe a denial so kindly, that the sting of disappointment was absorbed in the beauty of the declaration . . . [Washington did] not indulge the luxury of the sense, or the insatiate aims of ambition, but for the blessed purpose of disseminating love a protection of all. . . ." In short, Washington was a supreme example of the sympathetic and disinterested hero. The two traits are stressed in virtually all biographies of the Revolution's heroes during this period. "We have never contemplated the character of a magistrate more inflexible to wrong," wrote Williams, "nor of a man so active and so spotless, in any record, either ancient or modern; he did more for imitation, and less for repentance, than any contemporary. . . ."[3]

If the number of a book's editions indicates its appeal to readers, few biographies that followed the formula of recounting a hero's public accomplishments and then summarizing his moral traits were commercial successes. One of the few was Corry's *Life of Washington*, which received thirteen editions from its initial American publication through 1832. Perhaps most biographies in this mold did not sell well because of cost; essentially histories of the war, many tended to be long and, therefore, expensive. But even affordable biographies of the conventional sort did not attract buyers. For instance, Bancroft's pared down, less expensive version of John Marshall's *Life of Washington* attracted few buyers, even in federalist Massachusetts. American readers seemed to want something other than biographies written according to eighteenth-century literary canons. Weems, an Anglican minister who turned to bookselling in the 1790s, discovered what it was, and, in 1800, gave it to Americans with his biography of George Washington.[4]

Though Weems attempted to follow the dictates of eighteenth-century biographical writing, his first concern was to satisfy the preferences of southern book buyers, because meeting the needs of buyers meant more profit. One of Weems' assets, demonstrated repeatedly in his letters, was an ability to know what readers wanted. In 1799 he speculated that they would buy cheap biographies of the Revolution's heroes. Weems also knew that many of his customers were storytellers. Therefore, when he wrote his biography of Washington, he filled it with anecdotes. The stories present a world quite different from the realities of southern life. Social relations in Virginia, where Weems lived and most often sold books, were emotionally distant. Rivalry and violence were part of the fabric of society. In contrast to these actualities, Weems drew a portrait of society dominated by harmony, friendship, and affection. While the impetus for writing his *Life of Washington* was a desire for money, the anecdotes that give the biography its unique texture were a product of Weems' reaction to life in late eighteenth-century Virginia.

Weems gave readers memorable stories, yet kept the biography brief in order to hold down its price. Costing no more than one dollar, it was the most affordable biography of Washington available to Americans, although the book may have cost as much as a day's wages to a laborer of the time. Weems' highly unconventional *Life of Washington* became one of the bestselling books of the early nineteenth century.[5]

CONVENTIONS OF EIGHTEENTH-CENTURY BIOGRAPHY

Today's reader of Weems' *Life of Washington* is apt to be most struck by characteristics that set it apart from other biographies written during the early national period. Weems, however, did not think the work radically different from other lives of heroes. Though more affordable and entertaining than they, its form was similar to theirs, for Weems structured it according to the same literary conventions used by other biographers. Biographers viewed their work as a collateral branch of history and believed an individual life was comprehensible only as it related to the life of the community. William Johnson explained in the preface to his biography of Nathaniel Greene that "when the life of the individual becomes identified with the revolutionary history," it is imperative to use the war's events as a "framework in which to suspend" the hero's life. John Marshall asserted, "the history of General Washington, during his military command and civil administration, is so much that of his country" that Marshall's *Life of George Washington* "appeared to the author to be most sensibly incomplete and satisfactory, while unaccompanied by such a narrative of the principle events preceding our revolutionary war, as would make the reader acquainted with the genius, character, and resources of the people about to engage in that memorable contest." Sherburne's *Life of John Paul Jones*, Humphreys' *Essay on the Life of Israel Putnam*, and James' *Sketch of Francis Marion;* Caldwell's and Johnson's biographies of Nathaniel Greene; and Bancroft's, Ramsay's, Marshall's, and Jonathan Clark's lives of Washington were all, for the most part, histories of the military campaigns and public careers of their heroes.[6]

This kind of biography had its origins in classical antiquity and medieval hagiography. The notable classical precedent for biographers was Plutarch's *Lives*, the most popular classical reading of the time. In Plutarch's *Lives* is found a dictum frequently played upon in the eighteenth century: "*Longum eter est per praeepta, breve et efficax per exempla*, long is the way if we follow precepts, short and efficacious if we follow example." The immediate precedent in the tradition of hagiography was a seventeenth-century branch of scholarship that produced manuals on the lives of great men. Called *Artes Historicae*, the manuals differed in style and content, but were all explicitly pedagogical, with a stress on moral teaching. George Nadel has traced their development in England from Degory Whear, who occupied the first endowed chair in history at Oxford in 1622, through Hobbes and Bacon to Bolingbroke. In this tradition, the lives of great men interest the historian or biographer because they provide particular evidence in support of moral beliefs.[7]

In America, the most influential of the eighteenth-century proponents of exemplary history and biography was Henry Saint John,

Viscount Bolingbroke. The reader of American biographies, histories, magazines, and schoolbooks of the early republic finds a dictum Bolingbroke borrowed from Dionysus of Halicarnassus, "History is philosophy teaching by example," repeated with tiresome frequency. According to Bolingbroke, exemplary history allows images of virtues and vices to be drawn with clarity rarely found in life. Examples, "improved by the lively descriptions, and the just applauses or censures of historians," permit us "to receive our first impressions, and to acquire our first habits, in a scene where images of virtue and vice are continually represented to us in the colours that belong properly to them, before we enter another scene," adult life, where "virtue and vice are too often confounded, and what belongs to one is ascribed to the other." Repeated observation of clear examples of virtue and vice causes the viewer to follow those virtues "which example insinuated." It is for this reason "that the citizens of Rome placed the images of their ancestors in the vestibules of their houses: so that whenever they went in and out, these venerable bustoes met their eyes, and recalled the glorious actions of the dead to fire the living, to excite them to imitate and even to emulate their great forefathers." This design produced the intended effect, according to Bolingbroke. "The virtue of one generation was transfused, by the magick of example, into several; and a spirit of heroes was maintained through many ages of the commonwealth." Bolingbroke's remarks on the power of images to stimulate virtue need to be placed in the context of the ideas he develops in the "Letters on the Study and Use of History." Studying history, Bolingbroke argued, was important because it enabled one to learn the causes and effects of events and, therefore, provided the statesman a way of applying the past to the present. Additionally and more broadly, studying history provided, by analytical reasoning, a means to improve virtue. Simply looking at images of heroes may stimulate the desire to be virtuous, but it is not sufficient to improve virtue. Only analysis that exposed falsehoods, revealed truth, and eliminated prejudices would accomplish that end.[8]

Americans concerned with promoting virtue among the citizens of the new republic seem to have adopted the narrower idea that repeated exposure to images of virtue could "produce the habit" of imitating virtue. The Supreme Executive Council of Pennsylvania echoed Bolingbroke when it voted a resolution in 1779 to request Washington to sit for a portrait by Charles Willson Peale. The Council wanted to place Washington's portrait in its chambers "that the contemplation of it may excite others to tread in the same glorious and disinterested steps, which lead to public happiness and private honor." Samuel Stanhope Smith also drew on Bolingbroke's "Letters" when he told James Madison virtue could be recovered only by "recalling the lost images of virtue: contemplating them, & using them as motives of action, till they overcome those of vice again & again until after repeated struggles, & many foils they at length acquire the habitual superiority."[9]

Biographers who wrote lives of heroes of the Revolution during the early republic were practitioners of exemplary history. Their books took the same form: a narrative of a hero's public career was followed by a summary discussion of the exemplary moral traits that explained his rise to eminence. In this tradition, John Marshall's five-volume *Life of Washington* began with Cabot's exploration of the Americas, moved on to the founding of Jamestown, and continued through colonial history to conclude the first volume with a recounting of the French and Indian War. Volumes two through four concentrated on the military operations of the Revolution, and volume five examined the Critical Period and the years of Washington's presidency. In Marshall's work, Washington, defined as a realization of America's destiny, is devoid of any traits other than his extraordinary virtues. Reading the biography, one finds it is impossible to imagine Washington as a man. Even Marshall's description of the hero's physical traits is general rather than particular, abstract rather than concrete. Washington, he wrote, was "rather above the common size, his frame was robust. . . . His exterior created in the beholder the idea of strength united with manly gracefulness."[10]

Marshall concluded the fifth volume of *Life* with a customary description of character traits. Washington was "unaffected," dignified, "humane, benevolent, and conciliatory." He made "no pretensions to that vivacity which fascinates," and he possessed "that innate and unassuming modesty" which the "voluntary plaudits of millions could not betray into indiscretion." The virtue most admired by Marshall was Washington's "sound judgement and . . . discriminating mind." These constituted "the most prominent feature of his character" and enabled him to ponder any subject with "laborious attention." The adjectives might well serve to describe *Life* itself: judicious, discriminating, and, above all, laborious. John Adams aptly characterized it as a "mausoleum, 100 foot square at the base, and 200 feet in the air."[11]

To create his biography of Washington, Marshall followed a literary convention that had been supplanted in England for at least fifty years by a Johnsonian emphasis on private experience. Though Marshall's *Life of Washington* is admittedly an extreme example of the biographers' stress on collective history rather than individual experience, it was not unique. Biographers, including Weems, subordinated the lives of their heroes to the life of the new nation.[12]

Weems sold Marshall's work by subscription for C. P. Wayne of Philadelphia. He expected the biography would be a lucrative source of income for both Wayne and himself. Before Marshall finished the first volume, Weems told the publisher that, if the biography amply narrated Washington's life and gave "Old Washington fair play . . . [,] all will be well." A lively written work, handsomely presented would be especially beneficial to Wayne and himself. "I mean," he declared, "Let but the Interior of the Work be *Liberal & the* Exterior Elegant, and a Town house & a Country house, a coach and sideboard of Massy Plate shall all be thine. . . . God, I pray him, grant that this work may bring Moral Blessings on our Country . . . and wealth on C. P. W. & M. L. W." Unfortunately, the work did not fulfill either Weems' hopes for a lively biography or his prediction that Wayne and he would become wealthy by it. Potential buyers were put off by the biography's cost and its ponderous style.[13]

MASON LOCKE WEEMS AND HIS MARKET

Weems' advice concerning what was required to produce a popular biography had merit. An analysis of book inventories from post-Revolutionary Virginia estates reveals that the Bible was the most popular item in households. After the Bible, practical how-to books were most likely to be found in private libraries, with histories and biographies third in popularity. The parson knew what southern readers would buy. "Good Old Book," Weems wrote of the Bible, "I hope we shall live by you in this world and in the world to come." A master at understanding the book market, Weems continually tried to identify and cater to the preferences of book buyers. For example, when he was selling books for Mathew Carey, Weems attempted twice to establish bookstores whose stock would vary according to local tastes. Weems first developed the bookstore idea in the 1790s. The stores were to have been "distributed in every large neighbourhood, throught the State" and managed by "adjutants," merchants who were *"exemplary* for punctuality," and who could provide *"good securities."* Weems had thought this scheme promising, but had been cautious. Wanting only "to begin on a small scale and that by way of *experiment,"* Weems established a few stores such as the shop of Mr. Prentiss of Petersburg, who owned a "most excellent stand in the main street" from which to sell books. However, they did not prove lucrative and were only a minor part of Weems' selling activities at the time he and Carey ended their business partnership in 1801. When Weems and Carey resumed working together seven years later, Weems, convinced that a fortune was to be made by the bookstore plan, proposed that between 150 and 200 stores be established.[14]

The key to the success of this scheme, as Weems saw it in 1811, was to supply each store with books selected according to the preferences of the local inhabitants. The people of Virginia "differ widely in their political sentiments, and in their religious character, etc. etc.," he explained. "In one neighbourhood the Majority are *Methodists,* in another, *Baptists.* Here they cry out for Jefferson, there for Adams. Hence, Books, which in *one* place would go off *like a flash,* would in another be till doom's day on the shelves." Weems would tell Carey what stock to send to a store after passing through its neighborhood and making "acquaintance with the Political, Religious, Military & Agricultural character of the Inhabitants as would unerringly [lead?] to a choice of proper books." Weems wanted nothing but "the *sure card* ... ad captandum books,' that is, books which only suited the tastes of the people. These would include a full *"assortment of school books,* little Histories interesting & curious, Voyages, travels, fine Novels, &c. &c. &c."[15]

Weems' plan was never realized. Partly this was due to financial setbacks that prevented Carey from establishing the number of stores Weems thought necessary to make the plan a success. A more important reason for the plan's failure was that Carey sent the wrong kind of books; the stores' stock was not tailored to the markets Weems had defined.

This was an old story for Weems. When he first worked with Carey in the 1790s, Weems tried again and again to convince the publisher that books had to be suited to the southern market. Yet Carey, under pressure to sell off overstocked merchandise, continually shipped works that were without interest to Weems' buyers, such as religious tracts by New England divines. These books, which Carey wrote he had "promised in exchange, & purchased" from other publishers, "solely with a view to supply" Weems, were "as unsaleable in this State as Fiddles at Conventicle," lamented Weems. "You are perpetually complaining" about the absence of remittances, he wrote in March, 1798; yet Carey had no idea of "the globules of rich sweat I have lost as a result of "your oppressing and crushing me to earth by ten thousand puritannical books which as a good Catholic you know I did not request you to send, nay was eternally remonstrating against your sending. . . ." Southern book readers wanted their "pick & choice of fine Novels, entertaining histories, curiosity stirring voyages & travels," not the works of New England "Sable coloured Divinity," which Carey insisted on shipping to him. Weems said he considered "it a great misfortune that a man of my industry & spirits should have no better materials to work with . . . ; by loading me with such unfortunate books & writing such bitter letters, you have made me scratch my head oftener than I ever expected." Carey's shipments of high-priced books unknown to Weems' buyers caused the parson to indulge in incessant preaching about the "*Right books*." Because Weems' country was "made up of the small fry," he asked Carey to "Give me a Seine of small meshes" rather than expensive merchandise a seller might use to catch buyers in a more affluent market. "Give me," he pleaded, "50 Varieties, from 25 to 50 or 75 cents—*interesting subjects*—popular titles—fascinating frontispieces & showy bindings and carry everything before me— especially if to these you add the Auxillaries of numerous catalogues, & striking flourishes on the great pleasure & profits which the Farmers & their Boys & Girls may derive from education & Reading." If Carey would send books that might profit the reader, Weems insisted that he and Carey would profit also. Cheap books "conveying everything that the people here feel themselves interested in" would provide the publisher and bookseller with "an immense revenue." Carey did not heed these words when Weems wrote them in 1797 and 1809, nor did he follow Weems' advice in 1811 about supplying their stores with books that would interest readers.[16]

Weems' sensitivity to the preferences of southern readers alerted him in 1797 to the need for biographies of the Revolution's heroes. He wrote Carey, "the life of Gen. Wayne, Putnam, Green &c., Men whose courage and Abilities, whose patriotism and Exploits have won the love and admiration of the American people," would be a source of great profit. Carey was unmoved, however, and Weems did not raise the issue with him again until January, 1800, when he told the publisher, "I've something to whisper in your lug. Washington, you know is gone! Millions are gaping to read something about him. I am very nearly primed & cocked for 'em." He had a plan to present Washington's "history, sufficiently minute," and then to "go on to show that his unparrelled rise & elevation were owing to his Great Virtues." Weems was convinced that the book would sell because he had "read a part of it to one of my Parishioners, a first rate lady, and she wished I would print it, promising to take one for each of her children (a bakers dozen)." He thought Carey could print the work and "vend it admirably." Carey was not enthusiastic. Consequently, Weems himself arranged a printing of the work.[17]

WEEMS' BIOGRAPHY OF GEORGE WASHINGTON

The result was an eighty-page pamphlet, a mixture of historical chronology, anecdote, and sermon. Weems prefaced a Georgetown edition, published shortly after the biography's first printing, with a supplication to God to "grant us grace so to write, and read, and love, and imitate [Washington's] *Virtues*, that we may become a nation of Washingtons." Presenting the standard view of exemplary history, Weems asserted that "of all the means tending to accomplish this *best* of ends [the teaching of virtue], there is none like that of setting before them the bright examples of persons eminent for their virtues."[18]

Weems opened the *Life of Washington* in conventional biographical form by presenting a chronological narrative of Washington's public life. Much of this narrative concentrates on Washington's role in the French and Indian War. Weems relates how at the battle of Fort Necessity, which Washington surrendered to Count de Villiers, "never did the true Virginia valour shine more gloriously . . . to see 300 young fellows—commanded by a smooth-faced boy—all unaccustomed to the terrors of war—far from home . . . shut up in a dreary wilderness . . . [where] woods and rocks, and tall treetops, *filled with Indians*, were in one continued blaze and crash of fire-arms." Because of "such desparate resistance" on the part of Washington and his men, the French allowed them to "march away with all the honours of war, and carry with them their military stores and baggage."[19]

Weems's narration of the battle of Monongahela provides clearer instances of Washington's virtues. The army commanded by General Braddock was within seven miles of Fort Pitt on their march from Alexandria when they discovered Indians. Upon learning of the discovery, Washington, "with his usual modesty, observed to General Braddock what sort of enemy he had now to deal with. An enemy who would not, like the Europeans, come forward to a fair scuffle in the field, but, concealed behind the rocks and trees, carry on a deadly warfare with their rifles." Washington proposed that he be allowed to lead the Virginians to fight the enemy using Indian tactics. Braddock, however, "swelled with most unmanly rage. 'High times, by God,' he exclaimed, strutting to and fro, with arms akimbo, High times! when a young Buckskin can teach a British General how to fight!' Washington withdrew, biting his nether lip with grief and rage, to think how many brave fellows would draw short breath that day through the pride and obstinancy of one epauletted fool." Washington accepted the General's decision without protest, demonstrating of "that TRUE HEROIC VALOUR which combats malignant passions—conquers unreasonable *self*—rejects the hell of *hatred*, and invites the heaven of love into our own bosoms," even if it be love for one about to cause the deaths of hundreds of soldiers. Washington displayed the same kind of exemplary self-control once the battle began. Throughout it Washington remained calm and self-collected amid "the groans of the dying, the screams of the wounded, the piercing shrieks of the women, and the yells of the furious assaulting savages."[20]

Washington's heroic composure was not, however, the outward sign of an unfeeling man. He grieved for his men before the battle, knowing that so many would be killed, and throughout it sympathized with those about him who suffered. After the battle, when Washington learned that the French and Indians had killed families on the frontier, he was moved by the thought of "the unguarded Cabin—The father and the husband . . . weltering in his own heart's blood—while the wretched mother and her helpless little ones, with heartpiercing shrieks, and eyes wildstarting from their sockets, fly, but fly in vain."[21]

Weems continued to stress Washington's empathy and self-control in an obligatory discussion of character traits that followed the narration of the hero's public life. Discussions of character traits in conventional biographies were very brief, perfunctory listings of their subjects' exemplary virtues. Weems' discussion comprises nearly three-fourths of the biography. The unusual length came from Weems' practice of using anecdotes, to illustrate Washington's virtues. In one of the anecdotes, Weems told how Washington's sympathy for the poor caused him to distribute several hundred bushels of corn to them at a time of scarcity. Sympathy even led him to take pity on the fate of "wretched Cattle, which, driven out houseless and hayless into the cold wintry rains, presented such trembling spectacles of starvation and misery as were more than enough to state the tear into pity's eye." Sympathy was a supreme virtue because it was believed to be the basis of harmony among mankind; it was the bond which prevents the "fabric of all social order and happiness" from being torn apart. Weems described at the end of the *History* what a community without sympathy would be like. "Jealousy and hatred, true microscopes of hell, are before [men's] eyes and conceal from *each*, all the good *qualities* and *intentions* of the *other* and at the same time, so *distort, magnify,* and *blacken* all their designs and actions, that they appear to each other as little better than Devils." This is a hellish community. "Numerous Ravens, with ill-boding croaks and terrifying screams, are seen flapping their wings slow and sad over the fated city. All night long fearful noises are heard in the air, as of groans from dying persons; while frightful meteors, in the shape of fiery balls, shoot throught the gloom leaving long hideous tracks behind them like streams of blood." In the streets below, orators inflame men's passions "against each other to madness."[22]

In an anecdote about Washington's stay in Alexandria in 1754, Weems made clear the consequences of disregarding the feelings of others, and the vital importance of self-control. Stationed in Alexandria with his regiment, Washington went to the courthouse where he met a Mr. Payne, who supported for election to Assembly a candidate not favored by Washington. "A dispute happening to take place in the courthouse-yard" between Payne and Washington over the qualifications of the candidates for office "got warm." Washington did "a thing very uncommon with him"; he said "something that offended Payne; whereupon the *little* gentleman, who, though but a cub in *size*, was the old lion in heart, raised his sturdy hickory, and, at a single blow, brought our hero to the ground." Washington's regiment, upon "hearing how he had been treated, bolted out of their barracks, with everyman a weapon in his hand, threatening dreadful vengence" on Mr. Payne. Fortunately, Washington was able to calm the soldiers, after which he decided, "on mature reflection," that because his impudence had caused the exchange between Payne and himself, he would ask Payne for "his pardon on the morrow!" The following morning Washington summoned to his room Mr. Payne, telling him, *"to err sometimes is nature, to rectify error, is, always, glory. I find I was wrong in the affair of yesterday, you have had I think some satisfaction and if you think that sufficient here's my hand, let us be friends."*[23]

Examining this anecdote in his biography of Washington, Douglas Southall Freeman concluded that it is a "well founded" episode which occasioned Washington to decide that it would be a principle of his life to "receive reproof, when reproof is due, because no man can be readier to accuse me than I am to acknowledge an error when I am guilty of one, nor more desirous for atoning for a crime when I am guilty of one. . . ." To Washington the episode was significant for the lesson it taught about recognizing and admitting his guilt. For Weems, on the other hand, the confrontation between Washington and Payne was important because it exemplified the young hero's ability to control his passions. Had Washington yielded to them, he would have fulminated about the clash with Payne until he was in a "rage unutterable, while all the demons of hell, with bloodstained torches pointing at his bleeding honour, cried out revenge! revenge! revenge!" The result would have been the murder of either Washington or Payne in a duel, one of "Those tragedies which *cowards* create in society by *pusillanimously giving way to their bad passions."*[24]

A detail added by Weems to the factual account of Washington's confrontation with Payne transformed the incident into more than a personal dispute between two men. Washington's regiment was not in Alexandria at the time of the confrontation, yet Weems made the soldiers an essential element of the story. In the story, they take up arms to defend the honor of their commander, and threaten to throw "the whole town into flame," if need be, to correct the wrong done to their hero. Washington prevents this destruction from happening by regaining control of his passions and the passions of the regimental soldiers. Thus the additional fictional detail of the soldiers in the historical drama expands the scope of the confrontation from a private to a public incident, demonstrating the centrality of self-control for the governance of society.[25]

The crucial role that self-control has in the maintenance of social order and harmony is further emphasized by another device that Weems invented for his anecdote. The night before meeting Payne to offer his apology, Washington attended a dance. "No sooner had he made this noble resolution" to apologize, "than recovering that delicious gaiety which accompanies good purposes in a virtuous mind, he went to a ball that night, and behaved as pleasantly as if nothing had happened!" Washington's choice of activities is significant, for the dance was, in eighteenth-century Virginia, a highly important ceremony in which young and old, gentry and common folk, black and white, participated. It was, Rhys Isaac has noted, the "soul of the people," functioning "repeatedly as a common medium of expression, linking persons at opposite extremes of the social hierarchy. "Washington's attendance at the ball symbolically represents the return of social harmony after a momentary disruption in the order caused by the fight. "What sweet peace and harmony might for ever smile in the habitations of men," Weems exclaimed at the conclusion of the story, "if all had the courage to obey the sacred voice of JUSTICE and HUMANITY. . . ."[26]

This world of self-control and disinterested benevolence contrasts sharply with what we know of southern society in the late eighteenth century. Instead of social harmony and self-control, rivalry and violence pervaded southern life. Rivalry expressed itself in a variety of socially acceptable ways. One of the most popular was the quarter race, "a violent duel that tested not only the speed of the horses but also the daring and combative skill of the riders. . . ." The race-course was often a straightaway whose borders were defined by cheering spectators. Horseback riders competing in the race "were accustomed to jockey for position, and when the starter's signal sent them hurtling at full gallop down the narrow track, each might be free (depending on agreed rules) to use whip, knee, or elbow to dismount his opponent or drive him off the track."[27]

Abundant drinking often accompanied the races. An itinerant peddler traveling through North Carolina in 1807 visited Pyttsylvania, where "there we[re] a Number of People collected . . . to see quarter Races which they had that day and the Preceding one. Grog as usual had Great effect upon them and created much Noise (no fighting for a Wonder, neither was there any at Henry altho' the Noisyed Crew were _'s of them in a state of intoxication drinking out of tin Cups there being not a Single Glass upon the premises)—." Gambling was a more frequent competitive activity. Gambling could always be found at taverns, which were important centers of community life. A traveler through Virginia in the 1790s reported that on a visit to Richmond, "I had scarcely alighted from my horse at the tavern, when the landlord came to ask what game I was most partial to, as in such a room there was a faro table, in another a hazard table, in a third a billiard table, to any one of which he was ready to conduct me. Not the smallest secrecy is employed in keeping these tables; they are always crowded with people, and the doors of the apartment are only shut to prevent the rabble from coming in." At taverns, men also competed by matching wits. A visitor to a Virginia tavern experienced a "prolonged battle of wits between himself and 'a number of colone[l]s, captains, esquires &c, who had met . . . for public business.' Interspersed with loud guffaws, whereby the challengers shared their delight at their respective triumphs, were lines that indicated their skill in pressing provocation beyond permitted limits, and then seeming to step back, hold a pace, to within acceptable bounds. *Esq.* U: 'You lie, Sir, I mean on the bed.' To which the applauded answer from the butt of the humor was: 'And you lie, Sir, I mean under a mistake.'" When rules of etiquette that kept competition from turning into violent combat broke down, bystanders would surround the combatants, who fought "like wild beasts, biting, kicking, and endeavouring to tear each other's eyes out with their nails." An English traveler noted that, although the practice was made illegal by the Assembly, he had "seen a fellow, reckoned a great adept in gouging, who constantly kept the nails of both his thumbs and second fingers very long and pointed . . . [and] hardened them every evening in a candle."[28]

Intense rivalry was not confined to the racetrack and the tavern. Competition sometimes motivated southerners to build and furnish plantation houses. One gentleman lamented that his neighbor "built his fine home in Clarendon to beat me . . . [yet] I beat them in their own line—furniture, balls, & dinner parties." As this man's comment suggests, southerners also competed by opening their homes to guests. A Virginian of the late eighteenth century provided "five times as much as the men could eat" at a hunting dinner in order to match the meals his guests had served him. In his study of southern honor, Bertram Wyatt-Brown has observed that there "ran an undercurrent of deep mistrust, anxiety and personal competition" in the southern tradition of hospitality. The southern upper class also practiced the most violent of all rivalries, the duel. Though gentlemen were not above fighting one another with fists, in the late eighteenth century the duel became the preferred way to restore lost honor. Furthermore, by 1800 the duel was even being used to settle political disagreements. "At the election at Hanover courthouse, in the fall of 1800, Col. Mayo expressed his disapprobation of the policy of the last Virginia Legislatures. Col. Mayo . . . heard Mr. Penn call him a d——d rascal, and say he was not worthy to black the shoes of some of the members. Penn denied the 'd——d' but acknowledged the other, and a duel, next day . . . took place, Col. Mayo being slightly wounded."[29]

While the dispute between Washington and Payne reflected this atmosphere of competitiveness and violence, it also offered an alternative way of resolving personal differences. Like Col. Mayo and Mr. Penn, Col. Washington and Mr. Payne had political differences that erupted into verbal abuse and physical violence. Washington lashed out at Payne, who in turn struck the colonel. In similar circumstances, southern gentlemen of the early republic increasingly resorted to the duel to restore their honor. Washington, however, rejected the duel and demonstrated that the apology was equally honorable. Weems' anecdote was not merely the story of conflict between two men, but the dramatization of an alternative social ethos. On the one hand, men could relate to one another like Payne, as rivals compelled to resolve differences violently. On the other hand, they could, like Washington, acknowledge that true honor came only if one worked to achieve social harmony based on cooperation with others. Weems preferred the latter alternative and later wrote more anecdotes for the biography's revised edition to demonstrate what a world of social harmony might be like.

WEEMS' REVISION OF 1808

It is not clear whether Weems heard the new anecdotes about Washington during his bookselling journeys or created the anecdotes himself. He often attributes them to acquaintances of Washington. Weems writes, for example, that "an aged lady, who was a distant relative" of Washington recounted the story of George and the cherry tree, and claims that a "very aged gentleman, formerly a schoolmate" of the general, related that George disapproved of schoolyard fights. While it is possible Weems heard these and other stories from people who knew the hero, the attributions of authorship the parson frequently attached to anecdotes were more likely a strategy to lend authenticity to his work. Whatever the case, Weems' anecdotes were a brilliant accommodation to the southern audience's penchant for storytelling.[20]

Storytelling was an important means of transmitting cultural traditions in Virginia. Perhaps forty percent of Virginian society in the late eighteenth and early nineteenth centuries was illiterate. This population depended exclusively upon oral forms of communication. Storytelling, however, was not confined to the illiterate, for the oral tradition touched most Virginians. Availability of books other than the Bible was rare in rural Virginia, where most people lived. The childhood experiences of those who could read were formed by the oral culture of slaves, servants and other illiterate Virginians, as well as by the literate culture of family, friends and teachers. Virginians most readily acknowledged a man's good character if he "was an eloquent orator, enchanting storyteller, or witty raconteur." A strong tradition of storytelling existed among upper and lower class, literate and illiterate Virginians of the early republic. Weems, knowing that Virginians loved a good story, had included anecdotes in the biography from the start. In 1808 he strengthened the biography's appeal by adding still more memorable anecdotes about the nation's premier hero.[31]

Not only did Weems add more stories to the biography in 1808, but he significantly changed his conception of what kinds of stories were important to tell. His intention in the earlier biography had been to present Washington's "history, sufficiently minute" in order to demonstrate that "his unparalleled rise & elevation were owing to his Great Virtues." Stories of the hero's public actions had been examples from which Weems could derive precepts for readers to use to guide their behavior. In a new introductory chapter to the 1808 edition, titled *The Life of George Washington; With Curious Anecdotes, Equally Honorable to Himself, and Exemplary to his Young Countrymen*, he questioned the value of anecdotes about Washington's public achievements. "Have not a thousand orators spread his fame abroad," he asked before going on to answer, "Yes, they have indeed spread his fame abroad ... his fame as Generalissimo of the armies, and first President of the councils of his nation. But this is not *half h*is fame. ... True, he is there seen in *greatness*, but it is only the greatness of public character, which is no evidence of *true greatness* for a public character is often an artificial one." Those who achieve greatness in public life have not necessarily done so because they are virtuous; "even the common passions of pride, avarice, or ambition," can motivate a man to accomplish heroic acts which might appear, yet in truth would not be, exemplary. "But let all this heat and blaze of public situation and incitement be withdrawn; let him be thrust back into the shade of private life, and you shall see how soon, like a forced plant robbed of its hot-bed," the unauthentic hero "will drop his false foliage and fruit, and stand forth confessed in native stickweed sterility and worthlessness." Weems concluded that it "is not then in the glare of *public*, but in the shade of *private life*, that we are to look for the man. Private life is always *real life*."[32]

This is a Johnsonian conception of biography, clearly reflecting the view, stated in *The Rambler* essay No. 60, that "the business of the biographer is often to pass slightly over those performances and incidents, which produce vulgar greatness, to lead thoughts into domestick privacies, and display the minute details of daily life, where exterior appendages are cast aside, and men excel each other only by prudence and by virtue." To Johnson, the public aspect of a life was an "appendage" to the more central private life where the real character of a man could be found; an organic unity between the two remained. In Weems' conception, this organic unity was lost. Differences in the nature of public and private lives became a breach because public life could deceive and falsify. Only the private life was dependably "real."[33]

Perhaps Weems severed public from private life because his experience as a book seller made him wary of the dealings of other tradesmen. A year after writing his Johnsonian introduction to the *Life of George Washington*, Weems confided to Carey that "Constantly lecturing on philanthropy I came to think too favorably of others; and an early Liberator of my Slaves, I instinctively felt attached to Republicans. Hence I became the easy Dupe of honest weakness, It never once occurred to me, that a Printer who bawled and bawled for *Liberty*, like a Mullen, or a Prentiss, [booksellers with whom Weems did business] could be a Rascal. And the man who 'smiled & smiled' and invited me to dine appeared far too good to be capable of cheating me. But those days & delusions are all gone." Having suffered business losses from unethical men who appeared virtuous, Weems hesitated to seek the meaning of a man's life in his public behavior. The emphasis on private virtue seemed more judicious and rewarding to the biographer.[34]

Weems defended his new approach by arguing that while private virtues were "generally thrown into the background of the picture, and treated, as the grandees at the London and Paris routs, treat their good old *aunts* and *grandmothers*, huddling them together into the *back rooms*, there to wheeze and cough by themselves," they deserved a place in the foreground of biography because "they in fact were the food of the great actions of him, whom men call Washington." Furthermore, Weems argued that to stress the public actions of Washington would be to impede the instruction of virtues to children, for they could not hope to achieve what Washington accomplished and, therefore, would not identify with and imitate his virtues. To present Washington's public actions to them would be "like setting pictures of the Mammouth before the *mice* whom 'not all the manna of Heaven' can ever raise to equality." This too was a Johnsonian understanding of the value of biography. Johnson had argued that narratives of private virtues were "useful" because there is a "uniformity in the state of man" which enabled one to identify with and learn from an account of the private virtues of another. According to Johnson, "we are all prompted by the same motives, all deceived by the same fallacies, all animated by hope, obstructed by danger, entangled by desire, and seduced by pleasure." Weems, like Johnson, believed in the commonality of motives. He speculated that Washington's private motives would interest readers because everyone could find the same motives within themselves.[35]

Thus, in the revised version of his life of Washington, Weems put forward a view of biography that closely resembled Samuel Johnson's. Yet, its view of virtue was essentially different from the Englishman's. For Johnson, the private virtues were those hidden from public scrutiny because they were psychological states discernible only to the most sensitive observer. The truly important events of a life were "of a volatile and evanescent kind . . . rarely transmitted by tradition." To Weems, private virtues were those taught and practiced in the intimacy of the family, most especially those virtues taught and practiced at home.

Weems wrote of private virtue in anecdotes that concerned Mr. Washington's plan of education for George. One of the anecdotes told of an elderly woman who said that Mr. Washington once came to her door and asked my cousin Washington and my self to walk with him to the orchard, promising he would show us a fine sight. On arriving at the orchard, we were presented with a fine sight indeed. The whole earth was strewed with fruit: and yet the trees were bending under the weight of apples, which hung in clusters like grapes, and vainly strove to hide their blushing cheeks behind the green leaves. Now George, said his father, look here, my son! don't you remember when this good cousin of yours brought you that fine large apple last spring, how hardly I could prevail on you to divide with your brothers and sisters; though I promised you that if you would but do it, God Almighty would give you plenty of apples this fall. Poor George could not say a word; but hanging down his head, looked quite confused, while with his little naked toes he scratched in the soft ground. Now look up, my son, continued his father, look up George! and see there how richly the blessed God has made good my promise to you. Wherever you turn your eyes, you see the trees loaded with fine fruit; many of them indeed breaking down, while the ground is covered with mellow apples more than you could ever eat, my son, in all your life time.

Although Mr. Washington's lesson includes a lecture on God-the-father, the father of importance in this anecdote is Mr. Washington himself. When Mr. Washington reminds George of his sin, the boy does not ask for God's forgiveness, but gazes

in silence on the wide wilderness of fruit; he marked the busy humming bees, and heard the gay notes of birds, then lifting his eyes filled with shining moisture, to his father, he softly said, *"Well, Pa, only forgive me this time; see if I ever be so stingy any more."*[36]

Mr. Washington is vitally important not only because he offers George lessons about virtue, but because he is himself a model of virtue for the boy. A sequence of two anecdotes about Mr. Washington and his son makes clear the crucial role of the father's example in teaching the young hero virtue. One of the anecdotes is the famous story of the cherry tree; the other is a story Weems plagiarized from an English work.

In the familiar tale of the cherry tree, Weems tells how George, when "about six years old," was made the wealthy master of a *hatchet!* of which, like most little boys, he was unmoderately fond, and was constantly going about chopping everything that came his way. One day, in the garden, where he often amused himself hacking his mother's pea-sticks, he unluckily tried the edge of his hatchet on the body of a beautiful young English cherry-tree, which he barked so terribly, that I don't believe the tree ever got the better of it. The next morning the old gentleman finding out what had befallen his tree, which, by the by, was a great favorite, came into the house, and with much warmth asked for the mischievous author, declaring at the same time, that he would not have taken five guineas for his tree. Nobody could tell him any thing about it. Presently, George and his hatchet made their appearance. *George*, said his father, do *you know who killed that beautiful little cherry-tree yonder in the garden*? This was a tough *question* and George staggered under it for a moment; but quickly recovered himself. and looking at his father, with the sweet face of youth brightened with the inexpressible charm of all-conquering truth, he bravely cried out, "*I can't tell a lie, Pa; you know I can't tell a lie. I* did cut it *with my little hatchet.*" *Run to my arms, you dearest boy*, cried his father in transports, *run to my arms, glad am I, George, that you killed my tree; for you have paid me for it a thousand fold. Such an act of heroism in my son, is more worth than a thousand trees, though blossomed with silver, and their fruits of purest gold.*[37]

It has become a commonplace to associate the didactic message of this anecdote with George's remark, "*I can't tell a lie, Pa; you know I can't tell a lie.*" However, the public in Weems' time was apt to respond differently. Early nineteenth-century readers were likely to be as struck by the father's reaction to his son's confession as by the confession itself. Instead of punishing George for barking the cherry tree, Mr. Washington rewarded him with an embrace and the startling assertion, "*glad am I, George that you have killed my tree; for you have paid me for it a thousand fold.*" When Jonathan Clark used Weems' cherry tree anecdote for his *Life of Washington* (1813), he made the meaning of George's confession explicit by adding that Mr. Washington "was ever delighted with such instances of his son's attachment to virtuous principles. . . ." Clark understood that the father's reaction was an expression of joy at having successfully nurtured by example the virtue of honesty in his son.[38]

The anecdote immediately following this well-known story confirms that Mr. Washington's honesty is exemplary. Weems lifted the anecdote from James Beattie's commemorative account of his dead son. Beattie wrote that in order to determine "how far his son's reason could go in tracing out . . . the . . . first principle of all religion, the being of God," he planted seeds to spell out the initials of his son's name. Ten days later his son "came running . . . and with astonishment" told Beattie that "his name was growing in the garden." The father accompanied the younger Beattie to the family garden where, upon seeing the plants, the father declared "'I see it is so, but there is nothing in this worth notice; it is mere chance'." The son, of course, did not believe the event to be mere chance. Because Beattie's intention was to teach his son about God's being, he allowed his son to conclude that God arranged the plants so they would spell his initials.[39]

In Weems' variation of the Beattie anecdote, the father's role is more prominent. Mr. Washington plants seeds so they will spell "the full name of . . . GEORGE WASHINGTON" in order to "startle George into a lively sense of his Maker. . . ."

When George finds the plants, he asks how they happened to form his name. The father replies, as did Beattie, "'It grew there by *chance*, I suppose my son'." George, however, is not convinced. He asks, "How could they grow up so as to make *all* the letters of my name! and then standing one after another, to spell *my name so exactly!*—and all so neat and even too, at top and bottom!! O Pa, you must not say chance did all this." Whereas the young Beattie took the expected next step to conclude that only God could have caused the pattern to occur, George reasons that "*somebody* did it; and I dare say now, Pa, you did do it. . . ." At this, George's father smiles and confesses, "I indeed *did* it . . . to learn you a great thing which I wish you to understand. I want, my son, to introduce you to your *true* Father." Mr. Washington is unable to tell the lie that Beattie thought necessary to teach a theological lesson.[40]

In the earlier story of the cherry tree, George was imitating his father's virtuous honesty. Had George lied about the tree, the lie would have been proof of the father's moral failure rather than the child's, for one of the burdens placed on parents who taught by example was the responsibility for their children's lapses in virtue. Consequently, George's confession validated Mr. Washington's plan of education-by-example for his son.[41]

The reward for both successes—George's virtuousness and his father's instruction—was reaffirmation of affection between the two. George's sin of barking the tree was similar to Adam's fortunate fall, permitting George "to rise higher in his father's estimation than he had stood previously in his innocence." The incident strengthened the bond between George and his father, whom Weems called George's "best of friends."[42]

Friendship is an important theme in the revised edition of the biography. Weems stressed friendship in the only childhood anecdote whose setting was not the home. The story concerned George's ability to settle disputes among his schoolmates. Weems wrote that Washington's *"love of truth, and detestation of whatever was false and base"* made him a good friend of all the boys, who would call on him to settle disagreements over facts, for "his *word* was just as current among them as law." When disputes erupted into physical combat among boys, George would try to "disarm their savage passions by his arguments," and, if that failed, would "instantly go to the master" of the school. The gentleman who allegedly related this anecdote to Weems reported that "'the boys were often angry with George for this'—But he used to say, 'angry or not, you shall never, boys, have my consent to a practice so shocking! shocking even in *slaves* and *dogs;* then how utterly scandalous in little boys at school, who ought to look on one another as brothers.'" In *Life of Washington,* the practice of virtue became a means of gaining friendship. At school George carried "with him his virtues," especially his love for his schoolmates; although they may have been occasionally angry with him, a "gilt chariot with richest robes and liveried servants, could not half so substantially have befriended him" to them as his virtues did.[43]

Washington's knack of transforming opponents into friends, exemplified by his intervention into schoolyard disputes, was not lost as he grew older. Washington demonstrated the healing power of friendship when he was a young colonel in Alexandria. The anecdote of Washington and Payne began with discord which threatened to rupture the social harmony of the community, and ended by reaffirming the value of friendship, even among political opponents. Exercising self-control, Washington was able to restore order by offering Payne an apology with the words, *"let us be friends."* When the Revolutionary war erupted, he again demonstrated his ability to turn enemies into friends. He dispelled captured Hessians' "ill-grounded dread of the

Americans" by treating them "with the utmost tenderness and generosity." Washington's *"divine policy of doing good for evil"* in his relationship with the Hessians "melted down his iron enemies into golden friends."[44]

The 1808 revision of Weems' *Washington* emphasized the hero's affection and ability to make friends. In the original 1800 edition of the biography, Weems had most admired Washington's self-control and empathy, as stories about the battle of the Monongahela and Washington's confrontation with Mr. Payne illustrate. During the battle, Washington controlled his urge to criticize General Braddock's military tactics, even though the young hero anguished at the thought of the men who would die as a result of Braddock's mistake. At Alexandria, Washington refrained from continuing or escalating the rivalry between Payne and himself, and chose instead to conciliate. Both stories had stressed Washington's capability to restrain his passions and to sympathize with others. The new anecdotes Weems wrote for the 1808 edition elaborated the idea that empathy for others was critical for social harmony. In these stories, friendship replaced animosity or discord. The most famous of the new anecdotes, the story of the cherry tree, begins with a clash between father and son, and concludes with an outpouring of affection and conciliation. Other anecdotes repeated this pattern. At school and in battle, the Washington of these anecdotes transforms enemies into friends. In the new anecdotes, controlling anger and hostility becomes less important than expressing the love and affection necessary to achieve social harmony.

One comes away from these anecdotes feeling that they grew out of Weems' hopes and disappointments. Weems was disillusioned with men who called themselves Republicans, yet behaved in a way he considered ungentlemanly. He wanted to make Mathew Carey a friend, yet could never manage it. The failure puzzled him. Weems declared that he "often felt that joy which a man feels at the thought of a beloved brother" when he was with Carey, and never ceased "to feel a Joy in secret" at the thought of the publisher. Yet Carey never lived up to Weems' expectations. If Carey was sometimes a brother to the parson, he was at other times a "Barbarian." The word, an example of those "tropes & figures" Weems used to drive home a point, was an exaggeration that frustrated discussion of one of the many justified reasons for Carey's harsh letters. Nonetheless, it does indicate Weems' sentiment, a painful disappointment in his failure to establish an equal relationship with the publisher based on mutual affection. Given his failure with Carey and his disillusionment with men he did business with in the South, anecdotes about the virtues of disinterested benevolence and the value of affectionate bonds between individuals allowed Weems to describe a world he continually sought, but found only in the fictions of his life of Washington. Thousands of readers missing these values in their lives found the same kind of alternative in *Life of Washington* and made it an enormous success.[45]

"Domestick Subjects": Revolutionary Heroes in American Magazines

Until Boston and New York displaced it in the 1820s, Philadelphia was the publishing capital of the nation. Philadelphia printers issued book-length biographies as well as biographical dictionaries of Revolutionary heroes, including the Marshall's voluminous life of Washington and editions of Weem's popular biographies of Washington and Marion. Philadelphia produced many magazines of the period as well; between 1782 and 1800, biographical sketches and graphic portraits of Revolutionary heroes appeared largely in them, while Boston and New York, less active centers of publishing, issued several containing biographical sketches. Although southern magazines prior to 1800 were few, one included a portrait of George Washington and another a biographical sketch of Nathaniel Greene. After 1800, Boston equaled Philadelphia in magazines that had portraits, but Philadelphia's *Port Folio*, one of the few long-lived and financially successful magazines of the period, had the most ambitious series of articles and illustrations of Revolutionary heroes. Baltimore and Charleston magazines and, for the first time, one of the new western magazines, the *Ohio Miscellaneous Museum*, also devoted pages to the feats of the war's heroes.[46]

Magazine editors of the early republic picked over biographies and biographical dictionaries searching for tidbits to give their readers about the character and achievements of the Revolution's heroes. The choices were meager. The most savory pieces came from David Humphreys' popular *Essay on the Life of Israel Putnam*. Humphreys devoted much of the biography to his memoirs of the war years. The editors were more interested, however, in the biography's anecdotal first half. Putnam had told a friend, Albigence Waldo, stories of his childhood and his experiences in the French and Indian War, and Waldo passed them on to Humphreys. These stories, retold by Humphreys, appeared in several magazines of the early republic and became the first anecdotes of a patriot hero to be used in an American text.[47]

In addition to using Humphreys' stories of Putnam, magazine editors reprinted a few character sketches of Washington that originated in American biographies. Extracts from Weems' *Life of Washington* are not among this material. Although one reviewer observed that the parson's biography had "a kind of poetic fire running through every sentence . . . that irresistibly fixes the Attention, warms the Heart, and brings to the Eyes those delicious Waters which flow from Piety, Love, and Admiration," most critics disparaged the work. A reviewer for the *Monthly Anthology* complained that Weems' biography had "rotundity and bombast" mixed with "ludicrous quaintness." *Blackwood's Magazine* declared tersely, "It is full of ridiculous exaggerations." Weems' *Life of Washington* was too unorthodox to be a source for magazine articles on Washington. Given the paucity of suitable published material about Washington and other heroes of the Revolution, some editors wrote their own biographical sketches. The most important series of original sketches appeared in Joseph Dennie's *Port Folio* between 1809 and 1812.[48]

Sometimes biographical sketches were accompanied by graphic portraits of the heroes. The *Port Folio*, for example, included a portrait with each of its articles on Revolutionary War heroes. Portraits and biographical sketches could also be found together in other magazines, especially those that described Washington's accomplishments and character. However, portraits of the nation's foremost hero did not merely illustrate biographical sketches. Demonstrating their patriotism and responding to their readers' love of Washington, many magazine editors used graphic portraits of the general as frontispieces.

Written and visual representations of American heroes of the war were used by magazine editors who promoted national literature and arts. Soon after the end of the war, Mathew Carey declared that his *American Museum*, which printed a remarkable anecdote about Charles

Lee, would use American writings whenever possible. In 1787, the *Massachusetts Magazine*, which lauded Washington and Putnam, claimed that "a decided majority of our present Magazine is at least American." Character sketches and portraits of American heroes were an important part of the magazine's promotion of American culture. The growing nationalism of the period dictated that these "domestick subjects" were preferable to anything that originated in Europe.[49]

The American public's fervent patriotism matched the nationalism of magazine editors. An English traveler reported in 1818 that the *"national vanity* of the United States surpasses that of any other country . . . It blazes out everywhere, on all occasions—in their conversation, newspapers, pamphlets, speeches, and books." De Tocqueville observed an "irritable patriotism" that prohibited foreign visitors from criticizing "anything at all except, perhaps, the climate and the soil; and even then, Americans will be found ready to defend both, as if they had concurred in producing them." The atmosphere of fervent patriotism was reported by Weems also. He remarked on the "love and admiration of the American people" for American war heroes and noted that millions were "gaping" to read about Washington. As Weems discovered, offering the public biographies and portraits of heroes of the Revolution had financial rewards. The selling power of biographical and graphic portraits of Revolutionary heroes must have been apparent to editors of magazines in the early republic.[50]

GEORGE WASHINGTON

Editors gave biographical sketches of Washington a prominent place in their magazines. In 1789, Isaiah Thomas opened the fifth issue of the *Massachusetts Magazine* with a biographical sketch of the general taken from Jedidiah Morse's *American Geography*. The sketch, written by David Humphreys and used without attribution by Morse, praised Washington for the "virtuous simplicity" of his private life and for his "unvarying habits of regularity, temperance and industry." Two years later Washington again received prominence in the magazine when Thomas printed a biographical sketch of the general by John Bell. Bell's piece, which Weems drew upon to compose the first paragraph of his *Life and Memorable Actions of George Washington*, is notable for the connection it makes between Washington's physical demeanor and his character. "I would not mention to you the person of this distinguished man," Bell wrote, "were I not convinced that it bears great analogy to the qualifications of his mind." Bell may have been inspired to attempt an analogy between Washington's physical traits and moral character by John Caspar Lavater's *Essai sur la physiognomonie*. In his treatise on physiognomy, Lavater used graphic representations of Washington to analyze Washington's character. In 1788, a year before Lavater's essay was translated into English, the *Columbian Magazine* printed Lavater's analysis with a profile of Washington that bore faint resemblance to the hero (fig. 1). Washington's profile, Lavater observed, "indicates a sound judgement; freedom from prejudice, and a heart that opens itself to truth, which it imbibes and cherishes. It designates, likewise, taste, or if you please, a sense of beauty. The original must be distinguished by an indefatigable activity—a man who acts with prudence, and always with dignity."[51]

Bell, like Lavater, saw moral traits in Washington's facial features. "General Washington is a tall well made man, rather large boned, and has a tolerably genteel address," wrote Bell. "His features are manly and bold, his eyes of a bluish cast and very lively; his complexion sunburnt and without much colour, and his countenance sensible, composed and thoughtful." These characteristics suggested to Bell that Washington was "without much quickness," was "just, vigilant and generous," and was one who would never "exceed the bounds of the most rigid temperance."[52]

In addition to the brief biographies of Washington in the *Massachusetts Magazine*, the general received biographical sketches in two periodicals of 1806. One, the *Port Folio*, reprinted the concluding character description in David Ramsay's biography of Washington. The other, the *Literary Miscellany*, offered its own version of Washington's character. According to the *Port Folio* article, Washington "was uncommonly tall. Mountain air, abundant exercise in the open country, the wholesome toils of the chase, and the delightful scenes of rural life, expanded his limbs to an unusual, but well proportioned size. His exterior suggested to every beholder the idea of strength united with manly gracefulness." Yet, as impressive as Washington's physique was, the general's character was even more admirable. "The whole range of history does not present a character, on which we can dwell with such entire, unmixed admiration. His qualities were so happily blended, and so nicely harmonized that the result was a great and perfect whole." Specifically, Washington's integrity was "uncorruptible." Moreover, his "composition was all nerve; full of correct and manly ideas which were expressed in precise and forceable language." The *Port Folio* article concluded by listing out, one by one, Washington's virtues: his punctuality, honesty, temperance, hospitality, orderliness, piety, modesty, and equanimity. The *Literary Miscellany* of Cambridge, Massachusetts, observed that "Washington was a perfect example. . . . However, in him there was an "aggregate of excellence rather, than any glaring peculiarity. Withought those flashings of genius, which serve only to dazzle the understanding, the steady light of his intellect concentrated its rays to guide the progress of America to liberty and fame." In 1811, five years after the *Port Folio* and *Literary Miscellany* biographies, the editor of the *Literary Miscellany* of New York offered a sketch that repeated John Marshall's observation that Washington's life could not be separated from the history of the nation. "The life of this great and good man," the editor declared, "is so interwoven with that of our country, that to give even a perfect *sketch of* his political career, would far exceed our limits as well as ability." Nonetheless, the editor proceeded to chronicle in ten dull pages Washington's life from childhood to death.[53]

Engravings of Washington were in great demand. In 1809 Mason Locke Weems reported that he had an engraving of Washington "almost torn from me, such is the public feeling toward that great man." Engravings of Washington appeared in several magazines of the early national period. Two magazines that published biographical sketches of Washington accompanied them with the hero's portrait. The *Massachusetts Magazine* included with Bell's essay a profile portrait based on a likeness of the general by the English-born painter and engraver Joseph Wright, who is said to have drawn the portrait in 1790 without Washington's knowledge while the president sat in his pew at St. Paul's Chapel, New York (fig. 2). The *Philadelphia Monthly Magazine, or Universal Repository* (1798), used a masterful stipple portrait of Washington by H. Houston to illustrate an article about Washington by the magazine's editor, Thomas Condie (fig. 3). The portrait confirms Condie's assertion that copperplates published in the *Repository* would be "equal, if not superior, to the engravings that generally accompany Magazines." Condie's narrative, which he composed using the Humphrey/Morse and John Bell sketches, briefly takes Washington's life through the French and Indian War, continues with excerpts from Washington's journal, and concludes with Bell's description of Washington's character. The narrative does not match the virtuosity and elegance of Houston's print. Several magazines printed Washington's portrait as frontispieces. John Norman, one of the publishers of *The Boston Magazine*, and the engraver of its illustrations, created a remarkable portrait of Washington for the magazine's first volume (fig. 4). While Norman modeled Washington's face after an earlier portrait by Charles Willson Peale, he based the rest of the print on a French allegorical portrait of Montesquieu. At top-center of Norman's line engraving, a winged female figure holds a medallion portrait of Washington. She is bringing the portrait to the attention of a second figure who holds a lyre. Beneath the two figures, an angel blows a trumpet and Justice holds her scales. Norman explained that in the illustration "Nature stands ready to take the Lyre, while the Genius of Liberty presents a medal of the illustrious man who hath defended her standard in this new World—Fame blows her trumpet, and Astrea [Justice] finds a part of the earth where she may fix her residence."[54]

The first issue of the *Monthly Military Repository* (1796) opened with a frontispiece portrait of Washington by Elkanah Tisdale (fig. 5). Tisdale engraved beneath the portrait a small vignette of Washington taking command of the American army in 1775. One year after Tisdale's frontispiece in the *Military Repository*, the editors of the *American Universal Magazine* published what they believed to be a "truly elegant Portrait of the President," a frontispiece stipple engraving by Houston, who copied Joseph Wright's likeness of the general. The same year the *South Carolina Weekly Museum*, the only magazine at the time to be published south of Baltimore, included on its title page a crude woodcut portrait based on Charles Willson Peale's familiar image of Washington (fig. 6). After the turn of the century, Washington portraits also appeared as frontispieces in the *Connecticut Magazine* and the *Literary Casket.*[55]

Some portraits of Washington were didactic. Like John Norman's frontispiece for *Boston Magazine*, these used allegorical figures. One of the most elaborate was Alexander Lawson's engraving for the *Philadelphia Magazine and Review* (fig. 7).[56] The magazine's editor explained that the engraving was based on a display presented during a public dinner to honor Washington at Rickett's Circus in Philadelphia.

> At the expiration of his second presidentship, . . . Washington retired
> . . . . At this interesting period, the merchants of Philadelphia gave a

splendid public dinner in honor of the Statesman. . . . The company
. . . met at Oeller's hotel, and from thence marched in procession to
the place of entertainment. On their entering [Rickett's Circus],
WASHINGTON's march resounded through the place, when a
curtain was drawn up, and there was presented to view a transparent
full length *female figure*, as large as life, representing America,
seated on an elevation, composed of sixteen marble steps; on her right
side stood the *Federal shield and eagle*, and at her feet lay the
Cornucopia; in her right hand she held the Indian *calumet* of *peace*,
and in her left a scroll, inscribed 'Valedictory:'—in the perspective
appeared the *Temple of Fame:* on her left hand stood an *altar*,
dedicated to public gratitude, on which incense was burning; and at
the foot of the altar lay a plumed helmet and sword, from which a
figure of GEORGE WASHINGTON, as large as life, appeared
retiring down the steps, pointing with his right hand to the emblems
of power, which he had resigned, and with his left, to a beautiful
landscape, representing *Mount Vernon*, in front of which were seen
oxen harnessed to the plough. . . .[57]

The source for many of the elements in the entertainment described
and engraved in the *Philadelphia Magazine* was a popular emblem
book of the late eighteenth century, George Richardson's *Iconology*.
Published in 1779, Richardson's *Iconology* became a source of visual
imagery for English and American painters and engravers, including
John James Barralet, the designer of the entertainment at Rickett's
Circus. *Iconology* provided engravers with a language of visual
symbols that denoted a variety of specific meanings. Those familiar
with this language could "read" the message of an engraving. Using
Iconology as a lexicon, we may do the same.[58]

In her study of the eighteenth-century graphic portraits of
Washington, Wendy Wick has observed that Barralet's figure of
America resembles Richardson's emblem for peace. In Richardson,
Peace is represented by a female figure holding a cornucopia of fruit
and flowers, with an olive branch in one hand and a torch in the other.
The figure is setting fire to trophies of armor. But another Richardson
emblem seems a more likely model for Barralet's overall design (fig.
8). Richardson presented Britannia as a figure on a stepped platform at
whose base rests a cornucopia, a symbol of fertility. The figure holds a
spear in one hand and an olive branch in the other. Barralet presented

his America like Richardson's Britannia: in a similar pose, on a platform, with a cornucopia at its base. The use of Richardson's Britannia to represent America visually signified that the new nation had replaced the old as both guide and provider. Barralet drew other pictorial elements from *Iconology*. The plumed helmet and sword that sit at the feet of Washington recall Richardson's emblem for patriotism, in which a male figure stands upon a precipice with his left foot on a similar plumed helmet and sword (fig. 9). According to Richardson's lexicon, this signifies that patriots "fear no danger . . . and that their courage surmounts every difficulty."[59]

In addition to using emblems from *Iconology*, Barralet included a classical allusion in his design. In the background, oxen and a plow refer to Cincinnatus, who left his fields to defend his country and returned to the plow after fulfilling his patriotic duty. As Wick has noted, Barralet gave the overall design a particular American character by placing an Indian calumet in America's hand and by prominently including an eagle in the design's foreground.[60]

Allegorical symbolism occurred also in two magazine illustrations that used Washington's portrait to promote the American arts. Samuel Folwell, a Philadelphia engraver and designer of needlework, etched one of these illustrations for the *Philadelphia Repertory* of 1810. Like Barralet, Folwell composed his illustration using emblems from Richardson's *Iconology*. A figure seated in front of an easel closely resembles Richardson's allegorical figure, "Painting," whose medallion necklace signifies *imitatio*. According to the emblem vocabulary developed by Richardson and used by Folwell, placement of Washington's portrait on the easel signifies that the hero is a subject worthy of imitation. This interpretation of the engraving receives further support by Folwell's use of a second emblematic figure seated to the left of "Painting." This is "Fame," whose trumpet "signifies that the voice of Fame resounds like this instrument, and encourages men to imitate the virtuous."[61]

Two decades later, Washington's portrait occurred again in a setting with allegorical figures representing the arts. The title page of the ninth volume of the *New York Mirror*, a periodical that published many authors of the Knickerbocker literary school, used a steel engraving by Asher B. Durand (fig. 10). The engraving reveals Minerva placing a crown on a bust of Washington. Gathered around the bust, which sits on a pedestal, are allegorical figures representing music, painting and history. Durand gave these allegorical figures an American setting by placing Indians and Niagara Falls in the engraving's background.[62]

It is impossible to tell to what extent magazine subscribers were familiar with the emblem vocabulary used by engravers. We do know, however, that not all editors assumed their audience would be able to read the didactic message of an engraving. For instance, John Norman identified for readers the allegorical figures in his *Boston Magazine* portrait of Washington. When the *Port Folio* issued a framing print in 1811 that included an allegorical portrait and a character description of Washington, Joseph Dennie provided an interpretation of the engraving for the magazine's subscribers. Dennie explained that

> A rock secure in its strength amidst the fury and wild uproar of a troubled ocean, is a fit emblem of Washington unmoved by all the evils, dangers, and misfortunes attendant on civil and military life. It might also represent his example as the rock of our national safety, assailed as we are by whatever is insidious, or stormy, or dangerous. When in the discharge of his duty, like the *homo conscius recti* of the poet, though Nature had staggered in convulsions, and even tumbled in widespreading ruins around him, nothing could shake the firmness of his soul. The fair and stately evergreen supported by the rock, and withstanding the violence of a tempestuous sky, may well represent the purity of his virtue and the perpetuity of his fame; while the garland of oak-leaves encircling the whole, is a classical emblem of his civic worth.[63]

As tensions between the United States and Britain mounted in 1811, Dennie felt that "appearances almost justify an apprehension that Freedom will be forced to seek refuge in the skies." Because the "whole earth" might find itself "consolidated under a military despotism," Dennie thought it appropriate to gather together on the *Port Folio*'s pages "a few scattering rays from the glory of Washington, a name which has a wonder-working magic in the sound." Dennie's explication of the Washington portrait helped assure that the hero's glory would not be clouded by confusion about the engraving's meaning.

OTHER HEROES

Though magazine editors favored biographical and graphic portraits of Washington, they also published character sketches, anecdotes, and engravings of other Revolutionary heroes. The first of these to appear were an engraving and character sketch of Joseph Warren, who "fell gloriously in the trenches" during the Battle of Bunker Hill. John Norman, who created the *Boston Magazine*'s Washington illustration based on a French portrait of Montesquieu, engraved Warren's portrait. The portrait and sketch were published in the first volume of the magazine (fig. 11).[64] Two years later, in 1786, the *Columbian Magazine* included in its first volume a portrait and biographical sketch of Nathaniel Greene (fig. 12). Engraved by James Trenchard, the portrait may have been modeled on a painting of Greene by Charles Willson Peale. The portrait is displayed in an oval frame sitting on a platform with a cannon, cannon balls, a sword, drapery, palm branches, and laurel.[65] The biographical sketch, written by Mathew Carey, asserted that the general was "endowed with an uncommon degree of judgement and penetration, which, with a benevolent manner and affable behavior, acquired him a number of valuable friends."[66] In 1799, the biographical sketch by Carey, without accompanying portrait, appeared in the Richmond, Virginia, *National Magazine*.[67]

Humphreys' *Life of Putnam* was a source of anecdotes for several magazines. The *Columbian Magazine* and the *Philadelphia Repertory* reprinted the story of Putnam and the wolf, a tale some compilers of biographical dictionaries and schoolbook authors used. The story relates how Putnam moved in 1739 to Pomfret, Connecticut, where he found himself and his neighbors pestered by wolves destroying their sheep. "This havoc was committed by a she wolf, which with her annual whelps had for several years infested the vicinity." Putnam and his neighbors united to hunt it. Eventually they tracked the wolf down and drove it into a den. After several attempts to smoke out the animal failed, Putnam tried unsuccessfully to get his dog to rout it out. He then asked "his negro man to go down into the cavern and shoot the wolf; the negro declined the hazardous service. Then it was that their master, angry at the disappointment, and declaring that he was ashamed to have a coward in his family, resolved himself to destroy the ferocious beast . . . " Putnam took strips of birch bark, the only combustible material which he could obtain that would afford light in this deep and darksome cave, [and] prepared for his descent. Having, accordingly, devested himself of his coat and waistcoat, and having a long rope fastened round his legs, by which he might be pulled back at a concerted signal, he entered, head foremost, with the blazing torch in his hand. . . . [In the cave he] discovered the glaring eyeballs of the wolf, who was sitting at the extremity of the cavern. Starting, she gnashed her teeth and gave a sullen growl . . . [Putnam] kicked the rope, as a signal to be drawn up. The people at the mouth of the den, . . . supposing their friend to be in the most imminent danger, drew him forth with such celerity that his shirt was tripped over his head, and his skin severely lacerated.

Putnam entered the cave again with a gun and shot at the wolf. Unable to see whether he had killed the animal, he reentered the cave a third time. "Once more he came within sight of the wolf, who appearing very passive, he applied the torch to her nose, and perceiving her dead, he took hold of her ears, and then kicking the rope (still tied round his legs) the people above, with no small exultation, dragged them both out together!"[68]

In a three-part installment of Humphrey's biography of Putnam, the *Polyanthos* reprinted an account of Putnam's years during the last of the French and Indian Wars, and the Revolution. The extracts emphasized Putnam's bravery, selflessness, and humanity. During the 1758 battle for Ticonderoga, Putnam preferred "(if Heaven so ordered it) the loss of his own life to the loss of the lives of his brave associates." In a skirmish that left several hundred enemy dead, "Putnam's tender feelings taught him to regard an unfortunate vanquished foe, and to strive, by every lenient art in his power, to alleviate the miseries of war." Sympathy for his enemy caused the hero to remain "on the field of battle until dark, employed in collecting such of the enemy as were left wounded, to one place; and gave them all the liquor and little refreshments which he could procure; furnishing each with a blanket: under a French serjeant, who was badly wounded through the body, he put three blankets, and placed him in an easy posture against a tree." The story went on to point out that "the poor fellow could only squeeze his hand with an expressive grasp of gratitude. 'Ah,' said Major Putnam, 'depend upon it, my brave soldier, you shall be brought to the camp as soon as possible, and the same care shall be taken of you as if you were my brother.'" Unfortunately, Putnam's reassuring words were contradicted by the actions of Major Robert Rogers, who went into the field the following morning and "dispatched every one [of the wounded] to the world of spirits." Rogers, a *"civilized savage"* who concerned himself with military expediency, lacked Putnam's capacity to feel.[69]

The capacity to feel was also the subject of a story the *Ohio Miscellaneous Museum* published from Weems' *Life of Marion*. The story tells of a dinner of potatoes, which Marion serves to a British soldier. When the soldier realizes that the dinner fare is the norm, he exclaims, "Heavens and earth! then you must be in a bad box. I don't see, general, how you can stand it." Marion replies that "these things depend on feeling. . . . I'd rather fight . . . for my country, and feed on roots, than keep aloof, though wallowing in all the luxuries of Solomon." On returning to the British camp, the soldier looks so downtrodden that his commander asks why he is sad. "I have cause, sir," replied the soldier, "I have seen an American general and his officers, without pay, and almost without clothes, living on roots and drinking water; and all for LIBERTY! What chance have we against such men!" The execution of Colonel Isaac Hayne received a lengthy recounting and examination in the Charleston *Southern Review* in 1828. Hayne's patriotism had been questioned in Henry Lee's *Campaign of 1781*, and the editors of the magazine sought to restore the hero's stature as a martyr of the Revolution. The restoration was important. "We have always considered the moral and political lessons, taught by the history of the Revolution, as the most precious inheritance derived from our fathers," the editors wrote. "The exploits of our heroes—the wisdom of our statesmen, constitute a portion of our national wealth, which, we had fondly hoped, would have withstood the assaults of time itself." By attacking Lee's denigration of Hayne, the editors hoped to prevent Lee from removing one of the "most brilliant trophies of the Revolution."[70]

Anthony Wayne was the subject of biographical sketches and engravings in a number of magazines of the early republic. The *New York Magazine* included an engraving of Wayne with a memoir that urged readers to "remember that the man whose name is hereby revived in the public mind was thy friend." The writer reminded readers that Wayne "endured hunger, cold, pain, watchfulness, and fatigue, and he fought and bled, that thou mightest enjoy liberty and independence." The hero "died in a hut in the wilderness, remote from his friends, that his countrymen might enjoy in safety, beneath domestic shades, and in cultivated society, the peaceable fruits of their labours." The eulogist asked readers intending to travel to Erie, Pennsylvania, where Wayne died, to "stop and drop a tear in behalf of his country" over the hero's grave. "Plant near it a willow, which shall convey to it the dews of Heaven, and cut upon its bark, in letters that shall grow with time, the name of WAYNE, with the precious epithets, of PATRIOT, HERO, and FRIEND." Biographical sketches of Wayne appeared also in the *Polyanthos* and the *Port Folio.* The *Polyanthos* reprinted a sketch taken from a Boston newspaper a decade earlier. Although the sketch, which narrated the major events of Wayne's public career, was unexceptional, a stipple portrait by Samuel Harris presented an imposing military commander and gave the article attractiveness it would not have had otherwise (fig. 13).[71]

Beginning in 1809, the *Port Folio* printed the most extensive series of biographical sketches and portraits of the Revolution's military and naval heroes to appear in any magazine of the early republic. Portraits, most engraved by David Edwin, accompanied the sketches. For the October, 1809, issue Edwin engraved a likeness of Nicholas Biddle, a Philadelphian who died heroically at the age of twenty-seven when the ship he was commanding exploded during an engagement with the British frigate *Yarmouth* off Charleston in 1778 (fig. 14). Edwin also engraved for the *Port Folio* the most delicate of all the portraits of Anthony Wayne to appear in periodicals of the early republic (fig. 15), and provided the magazine with a representation of the medal that Congress had struck in honor of Horatio Gates. The medallion depicted Gate's portrait and a scene from his life. The medallion's obverse was a profile portrait inscribed "Horatio Gates Duci Strenuo" and "Comita Americana"; its reverse showed Burgoyne surrendering British troops to Gates at Saratoga. Novelist Charles Brockden Brown wrote the accompanying biographical sketch, which followed the convention of recounting public accomplishments and concluding with a summary of the hero's character traits. The Gates sketch was Brown's last work.[72]

In addition to his *Port Folio* engravings of Biddle, Wayne, and Gates, Edwin illustrated the magazine's biographical sketches of Daniel Morgan (fig. 16) and Henry Knox (fig. 17).[73] According to the author of the biographical sketch of Knox, the general possessed an abundance of "amiable virtues." Knox's "'heart was made of tenderness,'" declared the *Port Folio* sketch, and "he often disregarded his own wishes and convenience, in kind endeavours to promote the interest and happiness of his friends . . . Mildness ever beamed in his countenance . . . and equity and generosity always marked his intercourse with his fellowmen." The general's political beliefs interested the writer of the sketch most. "On the elevation of Mr. Jefferson in 1801," wrote the author of the sketch,

> [he] did not at first apprehend all the evils, nor did he speak with that severity of his political sentiments, in which some indulged themselves. Yet he ventured to predict, that so far as the new administration should differ from that of Washington, so far it would be found to be incorrect and injurious. "So long as the opinions and maxims of Washington have influence," he would often observe, "so long as his *real* political friends are permitted to direct the destinies of our country, so long shall we be independent, prosperous and free. But when his policy is exploded and his enemies bear rule, difficulties, dishonour and degradation will ensue."[74]

Similar political sentiments characterize the concluding remarks of Philip Schuyler's biographer in another issue of the *Port Folio*. Schuyler was a "practical man" who "never suffered soaring Fancy to disturb the balance of sober Reason." Because he was "too proudly honest to be indiscriminantly popular," and held in "utter abhorrence the intrigues of Democracy and the spirit of mob government," Schuyler had been attacked by the "envious, the ambitious and factious."[75]

Of the magazine editors who published biographical and graphic portraits of American military heroes of the Revolution, only Joseph Dennie had an explicit political agenda for promoting images of the heroes. When he proposed publication of the *Port Folio* in 1797–98, Dennie explained that one of the primary goals of the federalist periodical would be to "combat revolutionary doctrines." After Jefferson's election to the presidency, Dennie asserted that the magazine would be a torch in "this dark night of jacobinism." Whereas other editors included images of heroes in their magazines in response to the patriotism of their readers, Dennie's *Port Folio* engravings and biographical sketches of heroes of the Revolution were tributes to men who, according to Dennie and subsequent editors of the magazine, illuminated America with the light of federalism.[76]

Compared to biographies published during the fifty years following the Revolution, magazines that included character sketches or portraits of heroes had a significantly limited readership. The number of subscribers to even the most successful magazines was small in relation to readers of biographies. Because copyright restrictions did not exist and shoestring budgets prevented magazines from paying contributors, magazine editors freely reprinted extracts from biographies that praised the republican virtues of heroes. School texts such as readers and spellers of the period, the topic of the next chapter, also borrowed liberally from other sources to teach classical republican values. Unlike magazines, however, schoolbooks reached a much larger audience— children growing up in a post-Revolutionary society that was transforming the values the war's heroes embodied.[77]

Forming Republican Citizens: Schoolbook Accounts of Revolutionary Heroes

While biographers and magazine editors sometimes borrowed from other sources, most schoolbook authors of the early republic did nothing else. When they wanted a lesson about the virtues of the heroes of the Revolution, they took character descriptions and anecdotes from biographies, or used sketches of heroes that originally appeared in biographical dictionaries and magazines. Accounts of heroes began appearing in texts soon after the war ended. Nearly all texts were the product of New England Federalists. In 1789, Jedidiah Morse included in his *American Geography* a portion of David Humphrey's biographical sketch of Washington. In 1790, Noah Webster selected two anecdotes of heroism from Humphreys' *Life of Putnam* for inclusion in the *Little Reader's Assistant*. Although accounts of heroes of the Revolution appeared only in these two eighteenth-century schoolbooks, schoolbook sketches and anecdotes about heroes approximately doubled every decade from 1800 until 1830.[78]

During this time, the number of New England district schools, Sabbath schools, and academies increased notably, creating more demand for primers and readers. Schoolbooks, long a staple of New England printers, became a source of even more profit. In the 1820s and 1830s, schoolbooks accounted for nearly three-fifths of the sales of the Merriams, printers in rural Brookfield, Massachusetts. Most texts were reissued several times. Caleb Bingham's *American Preceptor*, which retold the story of Putnam and the wolf, went through 69 printings and sold an estimated 640,000 copies between 1795 and 1825. Biographical sketches and anecdotes of heroes of the Revolution reached more Americans by way of schoolbooks than by any other means.[79]

William Scott's *Lessons in Elocution* and Caleb Bingham's *American Preceptor* were typical school readers of the period. Both had a two-part structure. The first part presented rhetorical theory; Scott and Bingham instructed students on posture, gesture, articulation, and verbal expression. The second part consisted of short passages that students recited in class to practice rhetorical techniques. Passages intended for reading were also lessons in virtue. Children who had learned basic skills using primers continued their education by using Scott, Bingham, and similar texts to hone their reading skills and learn what were perceived as moral truths. [80]

Schoolbooks such as Scott's and Bingham's were staples in the inventory of printers and booksellers of the early republic. Weems, of course, was well aware of this. In an effort to tap the lucrative schoolbook market, he tried to establish his Washington biography as a school reader. He had some justification for thinking he might succeed. Although the biography did not concern itself with rhetorical techniques, it *was* full of examples of moral virtues. Weems hoped school children learning the importance of virtues would learn them from *Life of Washington.*

Weems' use of portraits of Washington in his biography was similar to the use of portraits by editors of magazines and biographical dictionaries. He included portraits because graphic representations of Washington were in great demand and increased the attractiveness of the book to potential buyers. This use of illustrations was quite different from that in schoolbooks. Although ornamental portraits of heroes were not wholly absent from school readers of the period, such portraits were uncommon. Instead of being decorative illustrations, visual images of heroes in schoolbooks most often took the form of the emblem. The emblem was composed of a graphic image, a narrative, or commentary on the ethical meaning of the image, and a brief statement of the emblem's moral. The emblem's didacticism suited it to the needs of schoolbook authors such as Noah Webster, who used the emblem form to present an illustration of Israel Putnam. By the third decade of the nineteenth century, however, schoolbook portraits of heroes were moving away from the didactic emblem form toward purely ornamental illustration.[81]

Schoolbook authors used sketches and anecdotes of heroes because they were brief enough, or could easily be made brief enough, to be used as reading lessons, and because they provided outstanding examples of virtues. Descriptions and stories about the Revolution's heroes also met the increasing demand to provide readers with American rather than European material. Authors tended to use anecdotes instead of the character sketches because they believed anecdotes had the rhetorical power to inculcate virtue in school children. This was an idea developed by eighteenth-century British aestheticians whose writings were popular in America. The formal characteristics of schoolbooks, American nationalism, and eighteenth-century British rhetorical theory influenced the kind and amount of material about heroes used in schoolbooks during the early national period.

THE NATURE OF SCHOOL READERS IN THE EARLY REPUBLIC

Like nearly all eighteenth and early nineteenth-century readers, William Scott's *Lessons in Elocution*, an English text used extensively in America during the early national period, and Caleb Bingham's popular *American Preceptor*, were collections of short extracts of poetry and prose taken from sermons, biographies, orations, poems and a miscellany of other kinds of writing intended to be used to teach reading and speaking. Schools continued the practice, begun by students at home, of reading aloud. Samuel Read Hall's *Lectures to School-Masters, on Teaching*, first published in 1829, insisted that the teacher devote his or her "whole attention" to the class when it is "called out to read," making sure that "every scholar" pronounces "every syllable so distinctly that you can hear and understand the words." Hall urged the teacher to take care that students "read with due degree of loudness, distinctness and slowness; and to regard the importance of accent, emphasis and cadence." Special care should be taken to assure that the class understands "the character of the lesson to be read" and that each student make "the manner and tone of the voice correspond to it." To achieve this correspondence between content and expression was to "enter into the feelings of the writer," and "to utter his words very nearly as we suppose he would utter them, if he were reading his own language to us." Hall encouraged teachers to give much of their time to developing these skills in their "scholars" because to "read with propriety and elegance is an interesting and valuable accomplishment."[82]

The first part of Scott's *Lessons* was devoted to an explication of rhetorical techniques that would help students achieve a proper and elegant style of reading. Scott's purpose was to teach students to describe "actions by words," a skill they could not learn by "leaving them . . . entirely to nature." Expressing conventional neoclassical thinking on the subject, Scott explained that "Improved and beautiful nature is the object of the painter's pencil, the poet's pen, and the rhetorician's action, and not that sordid and common nature which is perfectly rude and uncultivated. Nature directs us to art, and art selects and polishes the beauties of nature. . . ." Without instruction on the rudiments of reading aloud, students would, "in all probability, fall into very wild and ungraceful action." Scott hoped to avoid this outcome by teaching students a method of delivery "which shall not be inconsistent with the expression of any passion; which shall always keep the body in a graceful position, and shall so vary its motions, at proper intervals, to see the subject operating on the speaker, and not the speaker on the subject." To this end, Scott used a popular English schoolbook, James Burgh's *Art of Speaking*, to explicate in great detail body positions that correspond to stages of oral delivery and to summarize rules of elocution taken from John Walker's popular *Academic Speaker*. Likewise, Caleb Bingham opened his *American Preceptor* with an explication of rhetorical technique, although unlike Scott, who presented in great detail body positions and gestures, Bingham limited his remarks on gesture to general instructions.[83]

Having studied the methods of articulation and declamation outlined in the first parts of *Lessons in Elocution* and *American Preceptor*, students were prepared to read passages selected from a variety of sources. The second section of each reader was a collection of short extracts which students could use to practice rhetorical technique. Each passage was not only a lesson in reading, but also a lesson in moral virtue. First among these virtues was benevolence, a characteristic all heroes of the Revolution exemplified. Benevolence expressed itself in a variety of ways, but was characteristically revealed when an individual disregarded his own interest and promoted the interest of others. Examples of disinterested benevolence dominated readings in American texts. A lesson popular in many schoolbooks of the period explained that "if I seek an interest of my own, detached from that of others, I seek an interest that is chimerical, and can never have existence."[84] Like the "bee, the beaver, and the tribes of herding animals," each man and women was dependent on others for survival. Another lesson on benevolence compared human society "to a heap of embers, which, when placed asunder, can retain neither light nor heat, amidst the surrounding elements; but when brought together, they mutually give heat and light to each other; the flame breaks forth and not only defends itself, but subsides every thing around it." Consequently, it was imperative that each person show goodwill to others. "The security, the happiness, and the strength of human society, spring solely from the reciprocal benevolent affections of its members." The extraordinary benevolence demonstrated by those, such as Revolutionary heroes, who devoted their lives to securing the welfare of their countrymen gave them a special significance:

> The good husband, the good father, the good friend, the good neighbor, we honor as a good man, worthy of our love and affection. But the man in whom these more private affections are swallowed up in zeal for the good of his country, and of mankind, who goes about doing good, and seeks opportunities of being useful to his species, we revere as more than a good man; we esteem him—as a hero.[85]

Benevolence of a smaller magnitude was important also. It was especially necessary to be a dutiful son or daughter. "Honor thy father with thy whole heart," wrote Bingham, "and forget not the sorrows of thy mother. How canst thou recompense them the things which they have done for thee? It is a mark of a depraved mind to sneer at decrepid old age." A reading lesson on "Filial Duty and Devotion" pointed to the example of the stork, "which is generally esteemed an emblem of filial love" for the care it takes of its parents. Storks "live to a very advanced age"; their "limbs grow feeble, their feathers fall off, and they are in no way capable of providing for their own food or safety." When the old become disabled, however, their offspring care for them, "covering them with their wings, and nourishing them with the warmth of their bodies." They are a "striking example of filial duty," showing us that we ourselves must serve our parents in their old age, just as they once

served us in our youth. Scott, too, selected a lesson promoting respect
for elders. The lesson, which originated in the *Spectator*, told of an
elderly man, foreign to Greece, who attended a play and was spurned
by young Athenians. When he moved to a theater section reserved for
Lacedemodians, those citizens "rose up all to a man, and with the
greatest respect, received him among them. The Athenians being
suddenly touched with a sense of the Spartan virtue and their own
degeneracy, gave a thunder of applause; and the old man cried out, 'the
Athenians understand what is good, but the Lacedemodians practise
it."[86]

Sincerity and industry were promoted nearly as frequently as
benevolence in reading texts of the late eighteenth and early nineteenth
centuries. Sincerity was "the basis of every virtue," according to one of
Scott's lessons. "That darkness of character, where we can see no heart;
those foldings of art, through which no native affection is allowed to
penetrate, present an object unamiable in every season of life, but
particularly odious in youth. . . . Dissimulation in youth is the
forerunner of perfidy in old age." This sentiment was echoed in
Bingham's American text, which compared two students schooled
differently in the "Art of Pleasing." One, taught "in the school of
fashion," was ostensibly "all softness and plausibility, all benevolence
and generosity, all attention and assiduity." In truth, however, the
student possessed a "hard heart, meanness, selfishness, avarice, and a
total want of those principles from which alone true benevolence,
sincere friendship, and gentleness of disposition can originate." This
student, adept at a fashionable, but false way of pleasing, was compared
to another whose principles were based on "religion and morality." The
lesson noted that the "insincere art of pleasing resembles the inferior
species of timber in a building, which, in order to please the eye,
requires the assistance of paint; but the art which is founded on
sincerity, is more like that which displays far greater beauty in the
variety and richness of its own native veins and color."[87]

Selections from the writings of Hugh Blair and Benjamin Franklin
praised the virtue of industry. "Diligence, industry, and proper
improvement of time are material duties of the young," wrote Blair in a
passage selected by Scott for his *Lessons in Elocution*. Using an
argument that recalls Knox's "System of Virtue," the passage
exclaimed that industry was the "foundation of pleasure," for "Nothing
is so opposite to true enjoyment of life, as the relaxed and feeble state

of an indolent mind." Bingham extolled the virtue of industry by including in his text Benjamin Franklin's "Advice to a Young Tradesman" and an anonymous piece on the benefits of "Female Industry." While Franklin urged the young tradesman to remember that "the way to wealth . . . depends chiefly on two words, *industry* and *frugality*," the anonymous writer argued that "needlework, the care of domestic affairs, and a serious and retired life, is the proper function of women." These activities would enable women to avoid the fatal effects of "soft indolence, a stupid idleness, frivolous conversation, vain amusements, and a strong passion for public shows."[88]

These examples from Scott and Bingham do not exhaust the variety of lessons included in schoolbooks of the early republic, but they give the central issues schoolbook authors of the period addressed. Nearly every author promoted temperance, equanimity, benevolence, piety, sincerity, and industry. Nearly every one structured his text so students, by reading lessons about virtue, would be practicing the rhetorical techniques of oration. Rhetorical theory and technique defined the character of these texts. This had an important effect on the nature and use of schoolbook images of heroes of the Revolution. For one thing, pedagogical requirements for teaching rhetorical techniques dictated the length of passages included in schoolbooks. Because students practiced gesture, articulation, and verbal expression by reading passages aloud in class, schoolbook lessons necessarily had to be short. Consequently, schoolbook authors used brief accounts of heroes or shortened sketches and stories that were too long in their original form. Rhetorical theories about style also influenced the selection of accounts of heroes. In school readers of the early national period, rhetoric was the first concern; reading selections in texts promoted virtue, but the readings were above all instruments for teaching rhetoric.[89]

WEEMS' *LIFE OF GEORGE WASHINGTON* AS A SCHOOLBOOK

Though the form of Mason Locke Weems' *Life of Washington* differed radically from school readers, he sought to establish it as a schoolbook. There were always buyers for texts. When he was reestablishing business arrangements with Mathew Carey in 1809, Weems reminded the publisher, "You once told me that you heartily wished you had kept yourself to *schoolbooks*, in which event, you should, you said, have made a pound where you had made a dollar. If you could but view this business we are about to engage in, with my optics & impressions, you would never lose sight of School books—you would dig for them as for hidden treasures & pile them like Pyramids." In light of the growing hostilities between the United States and Britain, which would limit the availability of disposable income, schoolbooks would be a prudent choice for Carey to publish and Weems to sell. "War or no war," Weems observed, "People will have, because they must *have* school books," adding that if he and Carey concentrated on producing texts, they could get the schoolbooks "to contain just what Ethics & Politics we please."[90]

If his biography of Washington were used as a schoolbook, it would continue to sell regardless of the economic condition of the country. Seeking an endorsement of the biography, he sent Thomas Jefferson a copy of the seventh edition. He told Jefferson, "if, on perusing this private Life of Washington your Excellency should be pleased to find that I have not, like *some* of his Eulogists, set him up as a Common Hero for military ambition to idolize & imitate—Nor an Aristocrat, like *others*, to mislead & enslave the nation, but a pure Republican whom all our youth should know, that they may love & imitate his Virtues, and thereby immortalize 'the *last Republic* now on *earth.*' I shall heartily thank you for a line or two in favor of it—as a school book." In one important way, Weems' biography of Washington was similar to early American school readers: like them, it contained moral lessons by which Americans might guide their lives. Weems concluded both the 1800 edition and the 1808 revision of his biography with summaries of Washington's piety, patriotism, benevolence, justice, and industry. In a section devoted primarily to Washington's piety, Weems attributed the hero's military successes to his lifelong love of God. Weems claimed that several of Washington's acquaintances had seen him praying earnestly. One was a Quaker named Potts who unexpectedly came upon Washington at Valley Forge. Walking through the woods, "suddenly he heard the sound of a human voice. . . . As he approached the spot with a cautious step, whom should he behold, in a dark natural bower of ancient oaks, but the commander in chief of the American armies on his knees at prayer!" Potts ran home to his wife, declaring, "Sarah, my dear! Sarah! All's well! all's well! George Washington will yet prevail! . . . I have this day seen what I never expected. Thee knows that I always thought the sword and the gospel utterly inconsistent; and that no man could be a soldier and a Christian at the same time. But George Washington has this day convinced me of my mistake."[91] Washington's piety converted Potts from pacifism to the belief that one could without contradiction worship God and fight for one's country.

In addition to being pious, Washington displayed exemplary patriotism, "that divine cement of nations!" Outraged by attacks on frontier settlements during the French and Indian War, "Full-nerved with patriotic rage, he rushes upon the murderers of his countrymen, as the bounding lion upon the wretch who has invaded his brindled cubs." Later, at the outset of the Revolution, Washington "went forth the Leonidas of his country, resolved to fix her liberties or find a glorious grave. . . . At any period of this long conflict, he might no doubt have exchanged our liberties for myriads of shining gold, or highest seats of purpled honor." But patriotism moved Washington to defend his country. Washington was also benevolent, just, and honest. The hero's benevolence, "by spreading of his great virtues and talents the sweetly-beaming veil of goodness, rendered him at once the most endearing and venerable of human beings." His justice and honesty made him abhor slander and to buy only what he was sure he could pay for. "He said that he would rather take a turn on the rack than be sitting momentarily expecting to see the face of a creditor when he had no money to give him."[92]

Washington's honesty was "the cause of his, so amazing industry." Weems claimed that "of all the virtues that adorned the life of this great man, there is none more worthy of our imitation than his admirable INDUSTRY." Washington's industry was particularly notable because he had been born in a country "whose fertility and climate furnished both the means and invitation to vice." The notion that the southern climate bred vice was a recurrent theme of the eighteenth and early nineteenth centuries. As early as 1705, Robert Beverley argued that the southern climate and its "endless succession of Native Pleasures" encouraged laziness and indolence. The debilitating effects of the southern climate were asserted as well by Montesquieu, who argued in *The Spirit of the Laws*, a book well-known to educated Americans of the eighteenth century, that climate affected the mind, the body, and social institutions. The theme was repeated by later observers of the American cultural landscape. J. Hector St. John de Crevecoeur observed in his *Letters from an American Farmer* (1782) that the climate of the South "renders excesses of all kinds dangerous . . . the rays of their sun seem to urge [the citizens of Charleston] irresistibly to dissipation and pleasure. . . ." Weems' contemporary, David Ramsay, explained in his *History of the American Revolution* (1789) that "the New England provinces had improved much faster than others," for "it seems to be a general rule, that the more nature does for any body of men, the less they are disposed to do for themselves." Virginia and the Carolinas were thought too warm to produce men of virtue. In *History of South Carolina* (1809), Ramsay attributed the southern penchant for dueling and combative sports to the "warm weather and its attendant increase of bile in the stomach [which] has a physical tendency to produce an irritable temper." A cooler, more temperate climate was the "Proper nursery of genius, learning, [and] industry," remarked Hugh Williamson in his *Observation on the Climate in Different Parts of America* (1811).[93]

In spite of the handicap of having been bred in the South, Washington became a model of industry, surveying for his neighbors, tending his livestock, and managing his time in the most efficient and productive ways. Weems wrote that, like Alfred the Great, Washington "divided his time into four grand departments, *sleep, devotion, recreation,* and *business*," and that during "the hours of business . . . he would allow nothing to infringe." In camp

> no company, however illustrious; no pleasure, however elegant; no conversation, however agreeable, could prevail on him to neglect his business. The moment that his hour of duty was come, he would fill his glass, and with a smile call out to his friends around the social board, *"well, gentleman, here is bon repos,"* and immediately withdraw to business. *Bon repos* is French cant for good night. Washington drank it as a signal to break up; for the moment the company had swallowed the general's bon repos, it was *hats* and off."[94]

Weems attributed to industry the power to correct a variety of ills. It prevented, if not cured, sickness, for it "braces the nerves," and "purifies the blood"; *"rosy-cheeked industry"* assured that the "flame of life, bright and sparkling" burned in old age; and *"snow-robed industry"* made possible all the virtues, for it "preserves the morals of young men unsoiled, and secures the blessing of unblemished character and unbroken health." Because industry was central to moral and physical well being, and Washington possessed exemplary industry, Weems cried out: "O that the good genius of America may prevail! that the example of this, her favorite son, may be universally adopted! Soon shall our land be free from all those sloth-begotten demons which now haunt and torment us."[95]

Sloth was the archenemy of industry and the destroyer of nations. Sloth had caused David to saunter "*idly* on the terrace of his palace," enabling him to see "the naked beauties of the distant bathing Bathsheba. Lust, adultery, and murder were the consequences." Sloth "brought on ten years war between the Greeks and Trojans," and caused the suicide of "poor Mr. A___d," who, "having *nothing to do!* . . . strolled to a tavern, and to a card-table, where he lost his all!"[96]

Weems' sentiments were echoed in nearly every school reader of the early republic. One of Scott's lessons warned that although sloth "appears a slowly and flowing stream, it undermines all that is stable and flourishing. It not only saps the foundation of every virtue, but pours upon you a deluge of crimes and evils." Sloth is "like water, which first putrifies by stagnation, and then sends up noxious vapors, and fills the atmosphere with death." Elihu Marshall included in his *A Spelling Book of the English Language* (1830) a description of the sloth, because the animal was a "very just emblem of the slothful, who spend their time doing nothing, or that which is worse than nothing, while they ought to be improving their minds in virtue, and endeavouring to obtain those comforts, which render mankind happy."[97]

Perhaps the anecdotal quality of *Life of Washington* and its emphasis on moral traits helped promote Weems' book as a reader despite its unconventional structure. Although the book, a synthesis of conventional eighteenth-century biography and southern storytelling, was rambling and discursive, its many stories of Washington's life were adaptable to the short rhetorical lessons customary in schools. In this, Weems' biography was not far removed from more traditional texts like Scott's and Bingham's. Weems seems to have been at least partially successful in establishing his book as a school text. Reviewing Joseph Delaplaine's *Repository of the Lives and Portraits of Distinguished Americans*, a writer for the magazine *Portico* favorably compared Weem's *Life of Washington* to Delaplaine's work. The parson's biography, "a plain, unaspiring duodecimo" which could "be found in almost every school-room," wrote the reviewer, "will be regarded, by every true lover of true biography, with ten times more veneration, than the pompous quarto pages, which bear that title in the *Repository.*"[98]

ILLUSTRATIONS OF HEROES

Weems' biography of Washington was as unlike early nineteenth-century school readers in its use of relief cuts and engravings of the general as it was in its rambling and anecdotal discussions of moral virtues. Though John Wilmer used a frontispiece of Washington in *The American Nepos* (1805), and Noah Webster included a portrait of the hero in several editions of his speller, these were rare instances of decorative portraits in schoolbooks of the late eighteenth and early nineteenth centuries. Weems, on the other hand, used frontispiece portraits of Washington as often as he could, because they enhanced the salability of the books; titles printed with "fascinating frontispieces" were easier to market. In this regard, Weems did not differ from other authors and publishers of biographies, magazines, and biographical compilations of the period.[99]

Weems worked from the outset to assure his biography of Washington included a portrait of the hero. In June, 1799, he sent Carey a letter describing the new biography, "ad captandum gustum populi Americani!!!" In the letter, Weems sketched a rough portrait of Washington and asked Carey to order "a copper plate Frontispiece of that Hero, something in this way: George Washington Esqr. The Guardian Angel of his Country 'Go thy way Old George. Die when though wilt we shall never look upon thy like again." When Carey did not respond to Weems' request, and Weems arranged to have it printed by George Keatinge of Baltimore, Weems ensured that a frontispiece relief portrait of Washington be included in the edition. The frontispiece shows an eagle in flight, holding a medallion portrait of the general (fig. 18). Inscribed around the medallion's lower perimeter is "IMMORTAL WASHINGTON."[100]

In the early months of 1800, after Keatinge issued his edition, Weems continued to press Carey to publish another edition of *Washington.* He sent a manuscript of the biography, asking that Carey print it with "a beautiful likeness of Washington" taken from "one of the Ladies Magazines." Washington was, wrote Weems, "young beautiful and interesting when that was taken. If you have that engraved on Copper as a Frontispiece to our little book it might have a happy effect." Rather than Carey, however, the Philadelphia publisher John Bioren issued the biography's second edition. Bioren used a stipple engraving by Benjamin Tanner as a frontispiece (fig. 19). Based on Gilbert Stuart's "Atheneum" portrait of Washington, Tanner's engraving presented the hero in an oval frame that sat in a field of wavy, horizontal lines.[101]

For an unknown reason, Weems quickly tired of both this edition of the biography and its printer, whom he referred to as "Bioren, alias Black-Beard." By midsummer Weems had become "*dogsick, o n looking at*" the book, and asked Carey "to put to press an edition of the Life of Washington" that would use another portrait of the general. Weems did not require the portrait to resemble Washington, for he appears to have sent to Carey an engraving of General Hugh Mercer, suggesting it would be suitable for reengraving as a frontispiece for the Washington biography: "May it not do well to get this engraved for edition of Washington, altered for [from?] the Gallant Mercer [?]" To request that an engraving of one person be altered to create the portrait of another may seem strange; however, images purporting to be likenesses of Washington were not uncommon. Even though a portrait other than the one Weems recommended was used in the third edition of *A History of the Life and Death, Virtues and Exploits, of George Washington,* the parson was satisfied with the edition. For it Tanner engraved another, more finely executed likeness of Washington (fig. 20).[102]

Frontispiece portraits of Washington by Tanner and other illustrators were commonly included in later editions of the biography to increase the book's attractiveness to buyers. In addition to these portraits Weems urged Carey to have illustrations made of seven of the biography's anecdotes. He told Carey it would be profitable to have one of the plates engraved by the painter John Trumbull: "I have . . . an idea that you may with the aid of Trumbell [sic] get a Panorama of the Battle of Braddock. Trumbell could do it for you better than the Battle of Lodi. In that event thousands and myriads of dollars would be made. For not only all America, but England, Scotland and Ireland would rush to see a scene so terrific, and which would to all, become so *peculiarly,* I might say unexpressibly interesting because of the very awful part

taken in it by one so Dear to All." Weems concluded with this arrogant
advice for Trumbull: "The *historical* part (an hint for the Painter) may
be rendered much more terrible than it is." Although the plate used to
represent Braddock's defeat was far removed in style and technique
from Trumbull's work, the anonymous engraver of the seven plates did
model two scenes on Trumbull's paintings. One copied the painter's
Death of General Montgomery in the Attack on Quebec, and the other
imitated his *Death of General Warren at the Battle of Bunker's Hill*
(figs. 21 and 22).[103]

Unlike Weems' decorative portraits of Washington, schoolbook
illustrations were pedagogical. Most were closely related to passages
that students read. Together, illustrations and their texts taught moral
lessons, a practice that originated in the English emblem tradition. The
emblem comprised a picture, a commentary on the picture and a motto,
couplet or epigram that succinctly presented the emblem's moral.
Emblematists always began with a picture and interpreted each of the
picture's components in an attempt to determine its moral
implications.[104] Richardson's emblem commentaries, noted earlier, are
examples of the product of interpretation. The process itself may be
seen in the work of one of the first English emblematists, Geffery
Whitney (fig. 23). Whitney offered a relief cut depicting Sisyphus
rolling a stone across hilly terrain and accompanied the illustration with
the following commentary:

> Loe SISYPHUS, that rolls the restless stone
> To top of hill, with endless toil, and pain.
> Which being there, it tumbleth down alone,
> And then, the wretch must force it up again:
> > And as it falls, he makes it still ascend;
> > And yet, no toil can bring this work to end.
>
> This SISYPHUS: presenteth Adams race.
> The restless stone: their travail, and their toil:
> The hill, doth shew the day, and eek the space,
> Wherein they still do labour, work, and moil.
> > And though till night they strive the hill to climb,
> > Yet up again, the morning next betime.[105]

The verse beneath the relief cut of Sisyphus offers a point by point correspondence between the illustration and the moral idea Whitney wished to make: the figure of Sisyphus is equivalent to "Adam's race," the stone to man's toil, the hill to the time and place of man's work.

The emblem remained vital only as long as allegorical ways of thinking persisted, for the equivalencies emblematists established between picture and idea depended upon seeing the world symbolically. By the end of the seventeenth century, that way of viewing the world had waned. As a result, the emblematist lost his ability to derive moral commentaries from pictures. Rather than a source of meaning for the emblematist's commentary, the picture was reduced to a mere convention. No longer a part of the mainstream of literature, the emblem was relegated to amusements, children's moral tracts, and schoolbooks.[106]

The emblem convention determined the form of American schoolbook illustration from the start. Use of the emblem in American children's books began in the late seventeenth century with *The New England Primer*. To facilitate memorization, *The Primer* accompanied each letter of the alphabet with a rhyming couplet and a crude relief cut that illustrated the verse. From the beginning of the emblem's use in American schoolbooks, equivalencies of meaning between picture and verse that characterized the emblem at the height of its vitality were absent. *The Primer's* cuts and verses were emblematic in form only.[107]

Graphic representations of George Washington first entered American schoolbooks in *The Primer*. A late eighteenth-century edition replaced the original cut of a whale and its accompanying verse with a crude relief portrait of Washington and:

By Washington
Great deeds were done

A later Brattleborough, Vermont, edition offered another variation:

Great Washington brave
His country did save[108]

This picture-and-verse formula, a distant cousin of the English emblems, created one hundred years before, was repeated in a 1796 Germantown, Pennsylvania, edition of the primer (fig. 24). The

Germantown edition presented as its frontispiece a medallion portrait of
the hero with a commentary that advised readers to

> Love righteousness, ye that be judges of
> the earth: think of the Lord with a good
> heart, and in simplicity of heart seek him.[109]

A similar presentation of an illustration and commentary about
Washington occurred in the first history of America edited for young
children (fig. 25).[110] In this history of 1795, a couplet accompanying a
primitive relief cut of Washington explained that the hero was

> Great without pomp, without ambition brave,
> Proud not to conquer fellow-men, but save.[111]

Graphic portraits of Washington in *The New England Primer* and *The
History of America* conformed to the structure of the emblem. An
illustration of Israel Putnam that occurred in Noah Webster's *Little
Reader's Assistant* was also emblematic. In this text, which was
published in 1790, Webster repeated two stories about Putnam that
originated in Humphrey's biography of the hero, one of Putnam's
capture during the French and Indian War, and the other the tale of
Putnam and the wolf. The crude relief cut that accompanies the story of
the wolf shows Putnam supine in the cave where the wolf is trapped.
Below the illustration Webster has written the lesson's moral: "Such is
the effect of courage! Everyone who wishes to be a *hero*, must be as
bold as the brave Putnam" (fig. 26). The three-part structure of
narrative, illustration, and moral in this lesson about Putnam clearly
reflects the influence of the emblem on schoolbook illustrations of
heroes.

Two relief cuts in Samuel Griswold Goodrich's *First Book of
History* (1831) suggest that schoolbook illustrations of heroes were
beginning to lose their emblem form by the third decade of the
nineteenth century. Goodrich included in his text an illustration titled
"The Death of General Warren" (fig. 27), after John Trumbull's *The
Battle of Bunker Hill*, and a copy of Thomas Sully's *Washington's
Passage of the Delaware*. A glance at the two illustrations reveals that
they have none of the characteristics of the emblem. Placed amidst the
text, these relief cuts are purely ornamental embellishments for

Goodrich's book. They contrast sharply with the cut of Washington in the first published history for school children. Whereas that portrait included a couplet stating Washington's virtues, Goodrich's cuts merely illustrate the text's narrative. In its use of illustrations, *The First Book of History* resembled Weems' biography of Washington more than other school texts that contained graphic portraits of heroes of the Revolution.[112]

WRITTEN ACCOUNTS OF HEROES

The form of character sketches in biographies, biographical dictionaries, and magazines made them especially suited for schoolbooks; sketches describing the heroes' virtues were composed of brief paragraphs that could readily be extracted for use as reading lessons. The most popular were about Washington. From Morse's 1789 edition of *The American Geography*, the first schoolbook to contain a sketch of Washington, to the 1832 edition of *The National School Manual*, numerous school readers of the period contained litanies of Washington's character traits and virtues. On the other hand, pedagogical requirements often necessitated that anecdotes be modified. For example, Webster simplified the language and eliminated the details of Humphreys' original story of Putnam and the wolf. Other schoolbook authors did the same. Abridged versions of the anecdote occurred in Rufus Adams' *The Young Gentleman and Lady's Explanatory Monitor*, Albert Picket's *The Juvenile Mentor*, John Pierpont's *Introduction to the National Reader*, and Lydia Maria Child's *Biographical Sketches of Great and Good Men*.[113]

Schoolbook anecdotes of heroes dramatized virtues and cultural values that educators believed American children had to embrace if the republic were to survive. Foremost among these necessary virtues was disinterested benevolence. The virtue received one of its strongest expressions in Humphreys' tale of Putnam and the wolf. Though most authors edited Humphreys' story, John Wilmer and Caleb Bingham retained the richness of the original tale.[114]

The story of Putnam and the wolf taught children that an individual's ability to survive depended upon his or her bond to the community. The anecdote begins with an external threat to the community of Pomfret, the wolf. It had killed large numbers of livestock, causing "great havoc" by destroying the source of the farmer's livelihood. Various hunters had been able to kill the pups of the she-wolf, but they found the mother too wily to be caught by any one individual. Consequently, the farmers "entered into a combination" so that "two, by rotation," could be "constantly in pursuit" of the animal. Whereas attempts by individual hunters failed to ensnare the wolf, the combined effort of Putnam and his neighbors succeeded. Effective action to eliminate a threat to the community's survival was realized only when the community's members joined together to act.

Humphreys gave this belief in the interdependence of citizens a striking symbol in the figure of the rope that ties the hero to his neighbors. Set apart from them physically by his location in the cave and morally by his heroic willingness to risk his life, Putnam is nonetheless bound to them by the rope. Illustrations accompanying the story of Putnam and the wolf visually stress the rope's importance. The engraver of the illustration in Webster's reader translated Putnam's heroic stature into an oversized figure that dwarfs the townspeople outside the cave (see figure 26). A heavy white line representing the rope extends between Putnam and them. Just as the oversized figure of Putnam stresses his heroic nature, the thickly rendered rope visually emphasizes the hero's bond to the citizens of Pomfret. A more sophisticated relief cut of 1827 has, in an interesting way, lost this dual emphasis on heroic stature and the bond between hero and society (fig. 28). The illustration, which accompanied the anecdote in *Juvenile Miscellany*, diminishes Putnam to a childlike figure crouched in the den, his back turned to the viewer. The rope, on the other hand, is more prominent than in the Webster cut. In the *Juvenile Miscellany* illustration, the rope curls out of the right foreground like an umbilical cord, a visual reminder that as late as 1827 educators believed the individual, even if a hero, was inseparable from society.[115]

Putnam's heroic willingness to sacrifice his life to rid the farming community of the wolf dramatized a second cultural value. The citizen of the republic must, if called upon, be willing to "sacrifice his possessions, his dearest interests, his life itself" to save the community. The anecdote about Putnam and the wolf gave this value special emphasis by associating its opposite, an attachment to one's own life, with Putnam's servant. When the servant refuses to enter the cave because he believes the danger too great, Putnam labels him a coward. Thus, in the story, cowardliness became identified with low social and economic status. The effect was to bring to the reader's attention the association between virtue and Putnam's own status as master to the servant. The contrast between heroic master and his cowardly servant suggested by implication that those who were virtuous gained social and material benefits denied to those who were not. [116]

Historians of the American schoolbook have attributed the increase in the number of anecdotes about heroes of the Revolution to a rise in nationalism in early nineteenth-century America. [117] Yet the most popular of all American schoolbook anecdotes about a hero of the Revolution concerned the fate of a British soldier, John Andre. *Practical Reading Lessons on the Three Great Duties* (1830) gave children the particulars of Andre's mission and capture. "During the revolutionary war," the textbook explained,

> major Andre was sent by the commander of the British forces in New York, to communicate with the traitor Arnold, at West Point. Andre was in fact, a spy and as such, secretly, and in disguise, entered the American lines. After staying there long enough to accomplish the object of his visit [to arrange with Arnold the surrender of West Point], he set out on his return, furnished with a passport under the name of Anderson, signed by Arnold. He had proceeded some distance on his journey towards New York, when he unexpectedly fell in with three American militiamen, John Paulding, David Williams and Isaac Vanwert. They hailed him as usual, asked him who he was, where he was going, and what was his business. By shewing his passport, he might at once have escaped; but it seems that, in his momentary agitation and fear of discovery, he forgot it, and immediately offered his watch and some money, if they would let him pass. They smiled at the idea of being bribed, and proceeded to examine him, when they found concealed in his boot, a letter which completely disclosed his character, and the object of his visit to West Point. Again did he repeat his offers of money, and redouble his entreties. The three militiamen were inexorable. They conducted him to their commanding officer, who forwarded him to the commander in chief, when, after a regular trial and conviction, he was hanged as a Spy. [118]

To the author of *Practical Reading Lessons*, the story of Andre's capture exemplified the virtue of fidelity; it provided an illustration of faithfulness to one's country triumphing over the temptation of greed.

The virtuous militiamen Paulding, Williams, and Vanwert stood in contrast to Benedict Arnold, who sacrificed fidelity for greed.[119]

However, in most schoolbooks that told the story of Arnold and Andre, Andre himself was the virtuous counterpart to the villainous Arnold. The British officer's virtues displayed themselves most vividly at his execution. As several schoolbooks of the early republic told the story, when Andre was sentenced to die, the major declared that "he would be happy, if it were possible, to be indulged with a professional death; but the indulgence of being shot rather than hanged was not granted, because it was considered contrary to the custom of war." Andre only learned that he must die by hanging when he was taken to the place of execution.

> Upon seeing the gallows, he asked with some emotion, "must I die in this manner?"—He was told it was unavoidable. "I am reconciled to my fate," said he, "but not to the mode." Soon after, however, recollecting himself, he added, "It will be but a momentary pang"; and springing upon the cart, performed the last office to himself, with a composure that excited the admiration and melted the hearts of all the spectators.
>
> . . . Being told that the fatal moment was at hand, and asked if he had anything to say, he answered, "Nothing but to request that you will witness to the world that I die like a brave man."[120]

Andre's execution "excited a deep and general sympathy both among Britons and Americans." In a children's book devoted solely to the story of Arnold's treachery, "General H——," a veteran of the Revolution, relates the tale of Andre's death to a boy who exclaims, "Oh! . . . had it been *Arnold* instead of Andre!" The general responds by observing that the boy feels "as all felt, on that sad occasion—as all felt through America."[121]

The popularity of the story of Andre indicates that a hero's nationality mattered less to schoolbook authors than did his virtue. Because Andre's story vividly exemplified two important virtues, self-sacrifice for one's country and equanimity, schoolbook authors included the anecdote in their texts. This is not to say that schoolbook authors of the early republic were unaffected by the rising American nationalism. After the Revolution, authors increasingly used stories written by Americans about Americans to teach reading and virtue.

Nationalism, although not the sole cause of the growth in the number of schoolbook sketches and anecdotes about heroes of the Revolution, contributed to it. [122]

Nationalism may have motivated schoolbook authors of the early nineteenth century to create an American counterpart to Andre in the figure of Nathan Hale, a captain in the Revolutionary army who was executed by the British for spying. Hannah Adams was the first to offer a schoolbook account of this American martyr. In her abridged history of New England, Adams wrote that Hale, "animated by a sense of duty, and considering that an opportunity presented itself, by which he might be useful to his country," volunteered to infiltrate the British camp on Long Island. His mission was to determine the enemy's strength and plans. Hale was captured soon after reaching Long Island and was executed the morning following his arrest. He was "executed in a most unfeeling manner. . . . A clergyman, whose attendance he desired, was refused him; a Bible, for a moment's devotion, was not procured, though he requested it." Adams was careful to establish that Nathan Hale deserved as much admiration for his courage, patriotism, and equanimity as did Andre. "Should a comparison be drawn between Major Andre and Captain Hale," she wrote, "injustice would be done to the latter, should he not be placed on a equal ground with the former." She judged that it was Hale's "sense of duty, a hope that he might, in this way, be useful to his country, and an opinion which he had adopted, that every service, necessary to the public good, became honourable by being necessary, were the great motives" that caused him to undertake the hazardous mission. Adams spoke of Hale in terms that closely resembled early nineteenth-century commentaries on Andre's death. The story of Hale's capture and execution, noted Adams, "excites the most interesting reflections. To see such a character, in the flower of youth, cheerfully treading in the most powerful paths, influenced by the purest intentions, and, only emulous to do good to his country, without the imputation of a crime, fall a victim to policy, must have been wounding to the feelings even of his enemies." In short, Hale's motives and comportment were equal to Andre's. Furthermore, his last words—I am sorry I have but one life to lose for my country—were "superior to the dying words of Andre!" Schoolchildren could find in the story of Nathan Hale a model of virtue worthy of imitation. [123]

Of course, the most celebrated American hero in schoolbooks was George Washington. The most popular schoolbook anecdote of Washington was Weems' story of Washington and the cherry tree. The story began appearing in textbooks in the early 1820s. Within a decade, seven schoolbook authors had reprinted the tale, using it to exemplify the virtue of honesty. Some textbooks repeated the stories of Washington's bravery during the French and Indian War and his remarkable apology to Mr. Payne in Alexandria. Others used the legend of King Alfred and the Cakes. [124]

In the revised legend, Washington, disguised as a poor traveler, seeks shelter with a man named Jonathan and his wife, Tabitha. When the disguised Washington first appears at their home, Jonathan inquires anxiously, "What is become of our good general?" "Do you love him then?" asks Washington. "Love him?" Jonathan responds, "Every good man loves him. I kneel down and pray for him every night. You cannot love Washington better. . . ." Jonathan and Tabitha agree to shelter and feed the traveler as long as he will help with the domestic work. Jonathan asks, item by item, whether the guest can tie faggots, make brooms, chop wood, or bottom chairs. To each of these questions, Washington declares himself unable to perform the task. Finally he agrees to watch Tabitha's cakes, which are baking, while she and Jonathan go on an errand. When the couple returns, however, they discover the cakes are burned. As they begin to scold their guest for not fulfilling his promise, Washington reveals his identity. Mortified, they beg Washington's forgiveness, which he gladly offers. After the hero leaves, Tabitha wonders if her husband "could have thought it was the General?" "Why Tabitha," he replies, "we might have guessed he was born to be a General or some such great man, because you know he was fit for nothing else." Spoken without irony, Jonathan's comment gives the thrust of the anecdote. [125]

Authors told stories of lesser heroes' patriotism and courage in readers and in the schoolbook histories that began to appear in the 1820s. The hero's love of his country was exemplified in accounts of how Israel Putnam and Nathaniel Greene had responded to the news of fighting in Boston. In *The First Book of History*, Samuel Goodrich compared Putnam to Cincinnatus, the famous Roman patriot who left the plow to defend his country. Like Cincinnatus, Putnam "did not even stay to unharness the plow" when he heard that fighting had erupted between Americans and the British. Montgomery Bartlett declared in

The Common School Manual that when the Revolution came, Nathaniel Greene "laid off the wardrobe of Quaker cut drab, in which he had been educated" and "bared his arm in resistance to the British oppression." Although most military heroes experienced less dramatic transformations, all heroes were willing to commit their lives to protect their countrymen's liberty. Because of their willingness to fight for freedom, freedom, "in the hour of her need," gloried "in committing her cause" to them.[126]

On the battlefield the American hero showed exceptional courage. When Anthony Wayne commanded a detachment of infantry that conquered Stoney Point in 1779, he achieved "one of the most bold enterprises which occurred in the history of the war." Stoney Point, a British fort on the Hudson, was surrounded by a "deep morass" that Wayne had to lead his soldiers across to attack. "The English opened a tremendous fire of musketry and of cannon loaded with grape shot: but neither the innundated morass, nor a double palisade, nor the storm of fire that was poured upon them, could arrest the impetuosity of the Americans" led by Wayne. In the southern campaign, Nathaniel Greene, Daniel Morgan, and Henry Lee distinguished themselves by their battlefield courage. Greene always "displayed that cool, collective, and intrepid presence of mind and determined valour, which in the hour of danger, is ever present to a commander of the first order." His courage shown most brightly at the battle of Ninety-six, when he was "advised to retire, with his remaining force, to Virginia. To this suggestion, he replied, 'I will recover South Carolina or die in the attempt'." Daniel Morgan distinguished himself at the battle of Cowpens. "Morgan, with Herculean strength, hewing his way toward Tarlton, dealt death, in its most fearful form to all that opposed him." This hero's courageous fighting enabled the colonies to be "redeemed from British bondage," and to "march in republican simplicity, toward unparalleled greatness and happiness."[127]

The ultimate heroic act was to die on the battlefield. Two heroes who achieved this honor during the first year of the war became special symbols of patriotic courage and self-sacrifice. Joseph Warren, a Boston physician and political leader, died in the battle for Bunker Hill. Before his death Warren had "displayed great intrepidity in several skirmishes; had four days before been elected major general; and had, on the fatal day, hastened to the field of battle, to save his country as a volunteer. For his many virtues, his elegant manners, his generous devotion to his country, his high attainments in political science, he was beloved and respected by his republican associates; and to him their affection pointed as a future leader, in a cause dear to their hearts, and intimately connected with their glory."[128]

Caroline Matilda Thayer gave readers of her *First Lessons in the History of the United States* (1825) the details of Warren's death. "Finding his corps hotly pursued by the enemy, he despised all danger, and stood alone before the ranks, endeavouring to rally his troops and encourage them by his example. He pointed to their ensigns, and reminded them of their cheering mottos, 'Fight on, my brave fellows,' he exclaimed, 'the salvation of your country depends on this day's action. . . . Scarcely were these words uttered, when this distinguished patriot received a musket ball to the breast and fell dead on the Spot." Warren "fell covered with laurels, choosing rather to die in the field, than to grace the history of his foes by the triumph they would have enjoyed in his imprisonment." One schoolbook author discouraged readers from lamenting the death of Warren and other patriots who were killed at Bunker Hill. "Mourn not for them! They fell untimely, but they fell like stars of the firmament, and marked their radiant course with glory!" Richard Montgomery's death at the battle for Quebec was equally inspiring. In the assault on the city, Montgomery led his troops up to a "barrier or stockade of strong posts. Two of these he sawed off with his own hands." The hero then went forward "through the opening, encouraging his men to follow." At this moment a Canadian soldier fired a cannon, which was "instantly fatal to Montgomery, and to several favorite officers around him." One schoolbook author described Montgomery as "conspicuous, even in those times of enthusiasm, for his ardent devotion to the cause of freedom. He was endeared to the good, by the exercise, in the midst of war, of the amiable virtues."[129]

The courage of Warren and Montgomery, the disinterested benevolence of Putnam, the equanimity of Hale, the humility of Washington—how would those who had not experienced the war become as virtuous as these heroes? As the years passed, the older generation warned that the nation's youth were not living up to the ideals of those who had fought in the war. Educators such as Benjamin Rush and Noah Webster argued that children by nature were intractable and lacked virtue. Because popular virtue was thought to be part of the bedrock of classical republican society, it became increasingly imperative that the new generation learn to be as virtuous as the patriots of 1776. And the new generation would, educators believed, if children were "trained in the habits of thinking and speaking" which constituted Republican character. Anecdotes and sketches of Revolutionary heroes provided one way to engender these habits, for by reading stories of virtuous action the "virtue of one generation" would be "transfused, by the magick of example, into several; and a spirit of heroes would be maintained through many ages." The power of example, a common theme among all who wrote about Revolutionary heroes, took on special significance for those charged with educating the nation's youth.[130]

Portraits of Virtue and the Advent of Realism

When Mason Locke Weems wrote that of all the means of teaching children virtue, "there is none like that of setting before them the bright examples of persons eminent for their virtues"; or when the *Literary Miscellany* of Cambridge, Massachusetts, observed that "Washington was a perfect example" of virtue; or when the author of *The Columbian Preceptor* claimed that anecdotes of virtue had an ability to "exert an important influence on subsequent moral and intellectual character," each was asserting that images of heroes would inspire readers to act virtuously. Throughout the fifty years following the Revolution, this was an often-repeated refrain. Biographies of heroes were designed "to teach by example and experience . . . instilling into the tender mind the principles of liberty and a knowledge of the rights of man"; they had the ability to "furnish us with necessary example for the regulation of our conduct." Reading about heroes "fits us to be members of society." Biographers found specific, instructive examples of laudable actions in the "characters of persons who [had] acted conspicuous parts" in American history. Thomas Wilson spoke of his *Biography of Principle Military and Naval Heroes* (1817) as a "splendid monument" of the achievements of "the brave, the wise, or the great," asserting that "the faithful recital" of those achievements would be "a stimulus to the practice of virtue. . . ." David Ramsay offered his biography of George Washington "To THE YOUTH of the United States, in the hope that, from the EXAMPLE of their COMMON FATHER, they will learn to do and suffer whatever THEIR COUNTRY'S GOOD may require at their hands. . . ." The anonymous author of an article in *The Polyanthus* asserted that without the examples of the virtuous heroes who have preceded us, we would be like a ship owner who trusts his "ship to a school-taught pilot" instead of giving its command to one who knows by experience the course to steer. Man can know how to act, the writer continued without fear of mixing metaphors, only by looking into the "mirror" of virtuous example, for "it is in this mirror only, that he can perceive his own resemblance; here he learns to be shocked at deformity, and to be pleased with what is amiable; and thence he proceeds to dress his mind with every virtue."[131]

As Americans' ability to sustain the ideals of Revolutionary heroes came into question, the need to teach virtue became more pressing. To some, the country had become preoccupied with making money and accumulating wealth. The republican virtues exemplified by patriots appeared to be losing relevance. As David Ramsay explained, self-interest had "usurped the place of public spirit." Mercy Otis Warren lamented that she had written her *History of the Rise, Progress, and Termination of the American Revolution* "amidst the rage of accumulation" that was sweeping the country. "A preference of wealth to virtue is an alarming symptom," wrote a contributor to the *Richmond Enquirer* in 1810. "Honor, honesty, patriotism, virtue, yield without struggle to the potent powers of avarice. . . . A gold calf has stood up among us, and we have bowed down before the idol." In the face of this "love of gold," biographers, magazine editors, and schoolbook authors offered portraits of Revolutionary heroes as examples of republican virtues that desperately needed to be renewed.[132]

Anxiety increased as the older generation died. "Most of the actors in the scenes of those times have departed," noted the editor of the *Weekly Register* in 1811; "a new generation supplies their place. . . . Our youth should be taught to emulate their fathers—a race of men whose actions will shine more resplendent in history than aught that Greece or Rome can boast of. . . . Let the *American* lay his hand on his heart and ask himself, *'if they should be forgotten?'. . . ."* Charles Caldwell lamented in his *Memoirs of Nathaniel Greene,* "So marked had been our own indifference" to General Greene, and "so unrelenting our neglect, that they are a reproach to the nation." Thomas Rogers of Easton, Pennsylvania, published and twice reissued *A New Biographical Dictionary* with the hope that it would "rescue from forgetfulness the men who distinguished themselves in our glorious revolution. . . ." The writer of the *Port Folio*'s biography of Philip Schuyler "cast his eye over the present face of political society" in 1810 and found only a "Small, reduced, attenuated" number of worthy men. Many of the Revolutionary heroes had "descended to the tomb"; others had been "consigned to exile" from public life by their political opponents. "In a constellation so reduced, so thinly scattered," the writer observed, "the extinction of a single star creates an immense void." To forget was to give up freedom won by the Revolution. Describing an imaginary monument to John Dickinson, George Washington, and Robert Morris, several newspapers in 1782 printed an inscription warning readers to "Ask not their names. He is a / Slave who does not know them."[133]

According to the prevailing tenets of biography, reading about the exemplary lives of Revolutionary heroes instilled virtue. Misrepresentations of the patriots' achievements, which sullied portraits of their virtues, undermined the effort to reinvigorate republican values in the nation's citizens. Errors had to be corrected. In the preface to his biography of Putnam, David Humphreys explained that "falsehoods relative to the birth and achievements of Major General Putnam, which have (at a former period) been circulated with assiduity on both sides of the Atlantic, and the uncertainty which appeared to prevail with respect to his real character, first produced the resolution of writing this essay on his life." Claiming that "much of the fame that belongs" to Nathaniel Greene had been "arbitrarily passed to the credit of another," Charles Caldwell intended his biography of the general to be a "just though long neglected tribute to one of the most distinguished benefactors of our country. . . ." John Henry Sherburne assembled his life of John Paul Jones in order to present a true picture of the hero. "The character of John Paul Jones has been much misrepresented by those who have heretofore undertaken to write his life. They have, for the most part, depicted him as a plunderer, a pirate, cruel and unprincipled. . . . The present work, written from authentic documents, will redeem his name from the odium hitherto cast upon it." Getting the facts right was not simply restoring a hero's reputation. To misrepresent Revolutionary heroes was to attack the body politic of the new nation. As a writer for the *Southern Review* explained, "the exploits of our heroes . . . constitute a portion of our national wealth, which, we had fondly hoped, would have withstood the assaults of time itself." The writer went on to explain that attacks on the character of

Revolutionary heroes threatened to destroy the new nation's history. "It may be true, that our history, like all others, is 'of a mingled yarn of truth and falsehood,' but we fear, that any person who employs himself, at this day, in picking out the threads, will impair the beauty, if he does not destroy the strength of the fabric." Examples of wisdom and virtue such as those embodied in the lives of the war's heroes were the most important legacy one generation could pass on to the next; the examples would "confer the greatest blessings on posterity." By this logic, correcting erroneous accounts of the deeds and character of heroes could restore the body to health.[134]

There were those, however, who thought that the use of images of exemplary virtue to promote virtue had its dangers. A writer for the *Massachusetts Magazine* acknowledged that "example is superior to precept. . . . Precept is to example, no more than the representation of picture to the original, and the one has the advantage over the other, as much as the archetype exceeds the copy." Nonetheless, he warned that example had disadvantages, and it was "difficult to say whether its good or ill effects preponderate." According to the writer, example's primary disadvantage issued from the readers' tendency to "copy the faults [rather] than the excellencies of a character." This tendency was strongest in children, to whom examples were offered with the hope that instances of virtue would make them future virtuous citizens. The author explained, "there is no season in life" in which example "operates so powerfully as in youth; when fancy dresses every pleasure in the gayest robes . . . and gay temptation solicits every sense," examples of vices are apt to be more alluring than examples of virtue. For this reason, one educator reminded parents to permit their children to read only the most wholesome sketches and anecdotes. Parents "seem to forget that the lively imagination and the susceptible feelings of children are not less liable to be too much excited by the quality . . . of intellectual food they receive; and that their relish for the plain narrations of history, and the simple truths of science, may be entirely destroyed" if they are provided with books of the wrong kind. Parents must never give their children books "without constant explanation and application of the truths they contain and without ascertaining at every step the ideas they convey, and the impressions they produce." Indeed, as another critic pointed out, even examples of the right sort could be too powerful for children. "One of the greatest dangers of books written . . . by persons of talent is that of exciting the sensibility too powerfully. Books intended to inculcate the duties of obedience to parents, kindness to companions, respect for the rights of equals, industry, modesty, teachableness, &c., are apt to abound in strong cases" that are unsuitable for children. Consequently, the author recommended that parents replace stories of real heroes and heroines with stories about animals, "where a fabulous veil is thrown over the actors and sufferers, while the incidents and feelings are strictly human. . . . No parent would desire that a deeper sense of the reality of the circumstances, should lay hold of his child's mind."[135]

PSYCHOLOGICAL THEORIES OF EXAMPLE

Warnings about the detrimental effects of the force of examples had little impact on the creation of images of the Revolutionary heroes, even among schoolbook authors whose audience was believed to be most susceptible to harm. The power of example to elicit virtue was declared again and again by American writers and editors of the late eighteenth and early nineteenth centuries. In the decades following the Revolution, accounts of the extraordinary actions and admirable virtues of the war's heroes were offered to the public by men who had adopted from British thinkers, especially philosophers of the Scottish Enlightenment, psychological theories of how reading about virtuous behavior could engender virtue in the reader. In contrast to Bolingbroke, who argued that the analytical study of history improved virtue by improving the mind and ridding it of prejudice, these men— Joseph Addison, David Hume, Lord Kames, Alexander Gerard, Hugh Blair, and John Ogilvie—put forth treatises developing the idea that sensation apart from rational thought engendered virtue.[136]

Addison was one of the earliest to develop a psychological explanation of how images stimulate virtue. He declared his admiration for the writer who describes virtuous action "in so lively a manner" that his presentation of action becomes a vivid "picture" which the reader experiences as a "kind of spectator." Addison encouraged a lively style because it enabled the reader to feel "in himself all the variety of passion, which are correspondent" to the action described.[137]

Addison put his theory to work in *Cato*, the most popular play in America of the late eighteenth century. The play, which reflects the age's admiration of heroic death, dramatized the Roman hero's suicide in the face of bondage to Caesar. "How beautiful is death," Cato exclaims, "when earn'd by virtue! / Who would not be that youth [who died]? What pity is it / That we can die but once to serve our country." This sentiment greatly appealed to American patriots, and the play was often performed during the war. A death like Cato's was the ultimate sacrifice the patriot could make, for it demonstrated absolute allegiance to liberty. In death, as in no other circumstance, heroic virtue displayed itself. Cato was an example for all patriots. Like Juba, the Numidian prince who "forms himself to glory, / And breaks the fierceness of his native temper," they too could "copy out" Cato's "bright example." As Alexander Pope declared in the Prologue, the play offered Americans an opportunity to "Live o'er each scene, and be what they behold."[138]

During the eighteenth century other British thinkers whose work was well known in America developed theories of how readers and theater-goers could "Live o'er each scene, and be what they behold." The essential ingredient was sympathetic feeling evoked through vivid language. David Hume devoted a portion of his *Treatise of Human Nature* (1738–40) in an attempt to discover how the affections of others, virtuous or otherwise, influence us. We are so influenced, he concluded, if we "sympathize with others . . . receive by communication their inclinations and sentiments, however different from, or even contrary to our own." Earlier in *Treatise* Hume had distinguished between two different kinds of perceptions, which he called impressions and ideas. The former are perceptions immediately experienced; the latter are copies of immediately experienced perceptions, such as occur in thinking or reasoning. Hume distinguished these perceptions from one another by their differing degrees of vividness. "The difference betwixt these consists in the degrees of force and liveliness with which they strike upon the mind and make their way into our thoughts or consciousness. Those perceptions which enter with most force and violence we may name *impressions* and, under this name, if I comprehend all our sensations, passions, and emotions, as they make their first appearance in the soul. By *ideas* I mean the faint images of these in thinking and reasoning; such as, for instance, are all the perceptions excited by the present discourse, excepting only those which arise from the sight and touch, and excepting the immediate pleasure or uneasiness it may occasion." According to Hume, sympathetic communication begins when one person observes another's emotional expression. "When any affection is infused by sympathy," he wrote, "it is at first known only by its effects, and by those external signs in the countenance and conversation, which convey an idea of it." At first, the observer knows the emotion secondhand, by its external signs; that is, the observer knows it as an idea. However, he is able to experience the emotion itself if his idea of it becomes sufficiently vivid. When it does, it is transformed into an impression, and sympathetic feeling occurs. The "idea is presently converted into an impression, and acquires such a degree of force and vivacity, as to become the very passion itself, and produce an equal emotion, as any original affection."[139]

Hume argued that the difference between idea and impression, and therefore between dispassionate observation and sympathetic feeling, was a difference in "vivacity" or "liveliness" of perception. "The component parts of ideas and impressions are precisely alike," he wrote,

> The manner and order of their appearance may be the same. The different degrees of their force and vivacity are, therefore, the only particulars, that distinguish them: And as this difference may be removed, in some measure, by a relation betwixt the impressions and ideas, 'tis no wonder an idea of a sentiment or passion, may by this means be so enlivened as to become the very sentiment or passion. The lively idea of any object always approaches its impression; and 'tis certain we may feel sickness and pain from the mere force of imagination, and make a malady reality by often thinking of it. But this is most remarkable in the opinions and affections; and 'tis there principally, that a lively idea is converted into an impression . . . and 'tis after this manner we enter so deep into the opinions and affections of others, whenever we discover them.[140]

This concept of vivacity and its importance to sympathetic emotion influenced to varying degrees eighteenth-century British writers on aesthetics whose work became well known in America. Hume's most direct influence was upon Alexander Gerard, a professor of moral philosophy and logic who wrote *An Essay on Taste* (1759). Like Hume, Gerard believed lively impressions were necessary to stir emotion. However, to Gerard and subsequent writers on aesthetics, the creation of lively impressions was a literary concern.[141]

Gerard attributed a writer's failure to evoke sympathy to the abstractness of his language, and a writer's success to his language's particularity. "Present a mere abstract idea of good or evil," he wrote, and "the mind feels no emotion. Mention a particular advantage or disadvantage, desire or aversion, joy or sorrow is immediately roused. Tell us that a man is generous, benevolent, or compassionate, or, on the contrary, that his is sordid, selfish, or hardhearted; his character is too indefinite to excite either love or hatred. Rehearse a series of actions in which these characters have been displayed, immediately the story draws out the affections correspondent." Abstract language does not provide the details required to give a sympathetic idea its necessary vividness. "A very general idea is so unstable, that fancy cannot lay hold of it: but when a particular idea is presented, the imagination dwells upon it, cloathes it with a variety of circumstances, runs from it to other ideas that are connected with it, and finishes such a picture of the object represented by that idea, as will infallibly produce a suitable affection."[142]

In the popular *Elements of Criticism* (1762), Henry Home, Lord Kames, also stressed the importance of using vivid language to evoke sympathetic emotion. "The power of language to raise emotions, depends entirely on . . . raising . . . lively and distinct images. . . . the reader's passions are never sensibly moved till he be thrown into a kind of reverie; in which state, forgetting that he is reading, he conceives every incident as passing in his presence, precisely as if he were an eyewitness." Lively and particular language was capable of eliciting in the reader a desire to accomplish the virtuous actions that the language described. Wrote Kames, "let us figure some grand and heroic action, highly agreeable to the spectator: besides veneration for the author" of the heroic action, "the spectator feels in himself an unusual dignity of character, which disposeth him to great and noble actions. . . ." Kames called this feeling "*the sympathetic emotion of virtue,*" and argued that it could be achieved by describing "virtuous actions of every kind, and by no other sort." He recommended its frequent exercise by reading "histories of generous and disinterested actions, and frequent meditation upon them." Everyone who read vivid narratives of virtuous action could "keep the sympathetic emotion in constant exercise, which by degrees introduces a habit, and confirms the authority of virtue. . . ." Kames thought that with "respect to education . . . a spacious and commodious avenue to the heart of a young person is here opened" by this practice.[143]

Other eighteenth-century writers on aesthetics expressed similar thoughts on the power of vivid narratives to influence virtue. John Ogilvie argued that virtue is "almost constantly to be excited by holding up some standard of consummate excellence," as long as the writer's language is vivid enough to "add strength to the passion which ought to rise higher as the author proceeds." Ogilvie noted that the vividness with which images of virtue are given, the "circumstantial manner in which they are displayed, and our own propensity to extend our idea of the object until it is equalled with the illustration . . . operate so powerfully on the mind, as to suspend . . . reason. Transactions thus described become in fact so deeply interesting as to awaken in us the same passion that would have seized immediate spectators of the scene." Joseph Priestley asserted that a vivid description of heroic action "instantaneously and mechanically" caused the reader to take on the virtues described. The reader "enters into, adopts, and is actuated by, the sentiments that are presented to his mind. . . . Hence the passions, sentiments, and views of those persons whose history is written so as to engage our attention, become for a time . . . our own passions, sentiments, and views; and particularly, the accounts of the magnanimity, generosity, courage, clemency, & c. in our heroes, are read with a secret complacency and self-applause, arising from our indulging the same temper and disposition." Hugh Blair emphasized the importance of particular language. He argued that writers who wished the reader to sympathize with historical characters had to bring the particulars of action "into the most full and conspicuous light. . . . General facts make a slight impression on the mind. It is by means of circumstances and particulars . . . that a narration becomes . . . affecting to the Reader."[144]

THEORIES OF EXAMPLE IN AMERICAN EDUCATION

British arguments about the rhetorical power of images of virtue to stimulate moral behavior were part of the curriculum in colleges that trained men who later produced American reading texts. The prefaces of early nineteenth-century schoolbooks and educational journals occasionally paraphrased the theory. One educator asserted that vivid stories of moral acts were "unpretending, but powerful and persuasive teachers of wisdom." Another, speaking before the Themean Society in Schenectady, New York, declared that reading biographical anecdotes "was a powerful stimulus to every virtuous action" because the reader's "soul imbibes a sympathetic enthusiasm" for the stories' virtuous characters. As a result of this sympathetic feeling, the reader experiences all his "faculties aroused to action." Salma Hale, who created one of the earliest history texts, asserted that narrations of heroes of the Revolution could make lasting "virtuous and patriotic impressions," provided the narrations were written in a style that was "correct and pure" and "free from ambitious ornament." Fisher Ames offered the most forceful statement of the potential power of the vivid anecdote to influence moral behavior. In an oration on Washington that was later reprinted in many American schoolbooks, Ames claimed, "if I could paint [Washington's] virtues as he practised them, if I could convert the fervid enthusiasm of my heart into the talent to transmit his fame as it ought to pass to posterity—I should be the successful organ of your will. . . ."[145]

Schoolbook authors were concerned with the power of example for two additional reasons. For one thing, into the 1830s educators linked the survival of the republic to the virtue of its citizens. Charles Stewart Daveis, a New England lawyer, declared that in a country like the United States of America, "where the whole sovereignty is lodged in the people and all authority is exercised upon the strictest responsibility to the end of its universal welfare, *the education of the whole becomes the first interest of all.*" Noah Webster argued that children must be "trained in the habits of thinking and speaking" necessary for the development of a republican citizen. In his well-known *Plan for the Establishment of Public Schools*, Benjamin Rush asserted that education would "convert men into republican machines." To become educated meant both to learn skills such as reading, writing and arithmetic, and to develop the habit of virtue. Knowledge and virtue were "inseparable companions," Governor De Witt Clinton asserted before the State Legislature of New York; they were "in the moral, what light and heat are in the natural world—the illuminating and vivifying principle." Without knowledge and virtue, the nation's citizens would be misled. "The more ignorant the people are," a North Carolina newspaper observed, "the more they are subject to be led astray by erroneous opinions, to be deluded by misrepresentations, and imposed upon by artifice." Just as knowledgeable citizens were necessary for the health of the republic, virtuous citizens were essential for its survival. Without virtue, "a republic form of government cannot be supported—it cannot long exist."[146]

John Locke's *Thoughts Concerning Education*, a work that had a profound and far-reaching influence on American culture during the eighteenth century, also made the use of images of virtue desirable. Locke argued in the essay that the prevailing style of education based on coercion should be replaced with a pedagogy in which example had a major role. Locke agreed with traditionalists that parents and teachers needed to establish authority over children in order to educate them. Those who wanted "to govern their Children, should . . . look that they perfectly comply with the Will of their Parents. Would you have your son obedient to you when past a Child? Be sure then to establish the Authority of a Father, *as soon* as he is capable of Submission, and can understand in whose Power he is." But, unlike the old style of education, Locke's new pedagogy recommended against using "Imperviousness and Severity" as a means of establishing authority. Such methods were not appropriate because children were not animals to be beaten into obedience, but were rational beings who could reason and be reasoned with. Harsh discipline, such as flogging, was "but an ill Way of Treating Men, who have Reason of their own to guide them, unless you have a Mind to make your Children when grown up, weary of you; and secretly to say within themselves, *When will you Die, Father?*" [147]

According to Locke's epistemology, a child's mind is a *tabula rasa* upon which sense data are imprinted. All the "materials of reason and knowledge," Locke wrote in *An Essay on Human Understanding*, comes "from *experience*. In that all our knowledge is founded, and from that it ultimately derives itself." Some ideas are the result of direct sense perception; other, more complex ideas are reflections upon direct perceptions. Because all ideas were the product of sense perception, and all reasoning derived from experience, observing the behavior of others would determine the child's idea of virtue. Locke's epistemology made it imperative to expose the child during his formative years to appropriate examples of virtue.[148]

In a letter to Edward Clarke, Jr., for whom he wrote *Education*, Locke explained that

of all the ways whereby the children are to be instructed and their manners formed, the plainest, easiest, and most efficacious, is to set

before their eyes the examples of those things you would have them
do or avoid; which, when they are pointed out to them in the practice
of persons within their knowledge, with some reflection on their
beauty, or unbecomingness, are of more force to draw or deter their
imitation than any philosophical discourse can be made to them.
Virtue and vices can by no words be so plainly set before their
understandings as the actions of other men will show them, when you
direct their observation and bid them view this or that good or bad
quality in the practice.[149]

Locke urged fathers to do nothing before a son "which you would
not have him imitate" because he will "be sure to shelter himself under
your Example. . . . Nay, I know not whether it be not the best way to be
used by a Father, as long as he shall think fit, on any Occasion, to
reform any Thing he wishes mended in his Son: Nothing sinking so
gently, and so deep, into Men's Minds, as Example."[150]

There was another benefit to using example over coercion to
educate children. As a child grows older, Locke noted, and "Years
increase, Liberty must come with them; and in a great many Things he
must be trusted to his own Conduct; since there cannot be a Guard upon
him, except what you have put into his own Mind by Good Principles,
and established Habits, which is the best and surest, and therefore most
to be taken care of." The question was whether the child, when morally
independent, would both practice habits of virtue and maintain
affection for the parent. Locke argued that if coercion were used, the
former condition might prevail, but the latter surely would not. Virtues
would be practiced and affections continued only if example were the
method of teaching morality to the child. Indeed, the method of
teaching by example tended to develop rather than stifle the child's
affection for his parents. Locke assured the parent who used example to
teach a son, "so shall you have him your obedient Subject (as is fit)
whilst he is a Child, and your affectionate Friend, when he is a
Man."[151]

THE PORTRAYAL OF AFFECTIONATE RELATIONSHIPS

It is worth looking again at Weems' anecdotes about Washington in
light of this pedagogy. Weems' stories of the cherry tree and of the
cabbage seeds demonstrate the power of Mr. Washington's exemplary

behavior to teach the young hero virtue. Confronted by an angry father who has discovered the cherry-tree ruined, George confesses his guilt and is rewarded by an embrace. Mr. Washington cries out *"in transports, run to my arms; glad am I, George, that you killed my tree; for you have paid me a thousand fold."* George's confession is an *"act of heroism"* because he has the courage to do what is morally correct, even when faced with punishment. Yet, George is not punished because confessing the misdeed outweighs any harm the barking of the tree would do. Proof of George's honesty is *"more worth than a thousand trees, though blossomed with silver, and the fruits of purest gold."* The young hero had learned to be honest from the example of his father. The story of the cabbage seeds revealed that Mr. Washington himself was unable to tell a lie, even when the lie was benign and its effect beneficial. Mr. Washington planted the cabbage seeds in a pattern to spell out George's name in order to teach him that God was at work in the world. However, when George questioned whether it might not have been Mr. Washington rather than God at work, the father immediately confessed his role. The story of the cabbage seeds, which followed closely on the tale of the cherry tree, suggested that George learned to be honest from the example of his father.

Mr. Washington's method of teaching virtue had the effect Locke predicted in *Education*. Instead of growing apart, George and his father became "the best of friends." George also maintained a strong affection for his mother. Weems wrote that when the hero was fifteen years old he "felt the kindlings of his soul" to go to war. "The cause was this—In those days, the people of Virginia looked on Great Britain as the *mother country*, and to go thither was in common phrase, *'to go home.'* The name of OLD ENGLAND was music in their ears: and the bare mention of a blow meditated against her never failed to rouse a something at the heart, which instantly flamed on the cheek and flashed in the eye. Washington had his full share of these virtuous feelings. . . ." Yet, George's feelings for his biological mother were stronger than his attachment to his mother country. The young Washington procured a midshipman's berth on a ship of war and was about to sail for England, but "when he came to take leave of his mother, she wept bitterly, and told him *she felt that her heart would break if he left her.* George immediately got his trunk ashore! as he could not, for a moment, bear the idea of inflicting a wound on that dear life which had so long and so fondly sustained his own."[152]

Other heroes of the Revolution also voiced strong affection for their parents. Sergeant Jasper's thoughts turned to his mother and father when he was dying at Savannah, Georgia. Jasper first distinguished himself at the battle for Sullivan's Island off Charleston in 1776. As Weems relates the story in his *Life of Marion,*

> A ball from the enemy's ships carried away our flag staff. Scarcely had the stars of liberty touched the sand, before Jasper flew and snatched them up and kissed them with great enthusiasm. Then having fixed them to the point of his spontoon he leaped up on the breast work amidst the storm and fury of the battle, and restored them to their daring station—waving his hat at the same time and huzzaing "God save liberty and my country forever!"[153]

Three years later, Jasper again accomplished a heroic feat when he and a friend rescued from British imprisonment a man named Jones, his wife, and their child. Sympathy motivated the rescue attempt. Jasper and his friend saw that Mrs. Jones was in "deep distress." She sat, "A statue of grief . . . sighing and groaning the while as if her heart would burst . . . " because her husband was going to be hanged. The child, "seeing his father's hand's fast bound, and his mother weeping, added to the distressing scene by his artless tears and cries." After viewing this scene, "the tear was in the eye of both" Jasper and his friend. Filled with "tender-hearted sympathy," the two accomplished the rescue of Jones and his family despite being greatly outnumbered by the British.[154]

With such heroic feats behind him, Sergeant Jasper might have been expected to turn his deathbed thoughts to the contribution he made to win the war. Instead, Jasper thought fondly of his parents. Dying in the arms of Peter Horry, Weems' persona in *Life of Marion*, Jasper recounted hearing his mother "talk to me of God, and tell how it was he who built this great world, with all its riches and good things: and not for *himself* but for *me!*" Jasper affectionately remembered his mother taking him on her lap and telling him words that "went so deep into my heart, that they could never be taken away from me." In his dying moments, Jasper also fondly recalled his father. The sergeant asked Horry to give his "sword to my father, and tell him I never dishonoured it. If he should weep for me, tell him his son died in the hope of a better life."[155]

Filial affection received its most melodramatic expression in the story of the execution of Colonel Isaac Hayne. When the British captured Charleston, Isaac Hayne signed a proclamation declaring he would not contest British rule of the Carolinas. Hayne's reason for taking the oath mitigated this traitorous act: he loved his wife and children. "The heart of colonel Haynes [*sic*] was with his countrymen, and fervently did he pray that his *hands* could be with them too. But, these, alas! were bound up by his wife and children whom, it is said, he loved passing well. Helpless and trembling as they were, how could they be deserted by him in this fearful season, and given up to a brutal soldiery?"[156] But, when Cornwallis required Charleston men to fight against the American rebels, Hayne "was *compelled to fight* . . . He fled to his countrymen, who received him with joy, and gave him a command of horse."[157] Unfortunately, Hayne was soon captured by the British, who sentenced him to be hanged. Hayne's bravery throughout the trial, imprisonment, and execution was exemplary. "On his cheek alone, all agree," the ordeal "produced no change." The colonel's equanimity contrasted dramatically with his thirteen year-old son's reactions to the events (fig. 29). The son stayed with Hayne in prison, where he "beheld his . . . beloved father, in the power of his enemies, loaded with irons and condemned to die . . . he sat continually by his father's side, and looked at him with eyes so piercing sad, as often wrung tears of blood from his heart." The father spoke frequently with his son, trying to "fortify him against the sad trial that was at hand." The morning of Hayne's execution, his son went with him to the gallows.

Soon as they came in sight of the gallows, the father strengthened himself and said,— "*now, my son, shew yourself a man! That tree is the boundary of my life, and of all my life's sorrows. Beyond that, the wicked cease from troubling and the weary are at rest. Don't lay too much to heart [my] separation from you: it will be but short. . . . Today I die. And you, my son, though but young, must shortly follow. . . .*"

"Yes, my father," replied the broken-hearted youth, "I shall shortly follow you: for indeed I feel that I cannot live long."[158]

And the boy did not live long afterward. When he saw his father hanged, the boy "stood like one transfixed and motionless with horror."

Intense grief "like a fever, burnt inwardly and scorched his brain, for he became indifferent to every thing around him, and often wandered as one disordered in his kind . . . He died insane, and in his last moments often called on the name of his father, in terms that brought tears to the hardest hearts."[159]

With this story, Weems created a hero not only in Colonel Hayne, but also in the figure of the colonel's son. Hayne was a hero because he was patriotic, willing to die for his country, and able to die with equanimity. The son's heroism, on the other hand, issued from his intense affection for his father, which he exemplified by first falling apart and then dying of grief.

Affection between husbands and wives was also prominent in images of heroes of the Revolution. The story of "poor Peter Yarnall" and his wife in Weems' biography of Marion illustrates how marital affections were a central part of the heroic image. Like Hayne, Yarnall was a reluctant participant in the war. A Quaker, he agreed hesitantly to stand guard over loyalist prisoners for a moment while the regular watchman went on an errand. According to Weems' account, the British heard of Yarnall's act and arrested him. "Vain were all his own explanations, his wife's entreties, or his children's cries"; Yarnall was taken to prison, where his wife and fifteen year-old daughter visited him daily. On the fourth day of his captivity, Yarnall was without warning hanged. Upon seeing him "hung dead on a beam" his daughter "sunk to the ground; but her mother, as if petrified at the sight, stood silent and motionless, gazing on her dead husband with that wild keen eye of unutterable woe, which pierces all hearts." She quickly recovered enough to remove her husband's body, and remained composed until Yarnall was buried. "But soon as the grave had shut its mouth on her husband, and divorced him for ever from her sight, the remembrance of the past rushed upon her thoughts with a weight too heavy for her feeble nature to bear. Then clasping her hands in agony, she shrieked out 'Poor me! poor me! I have no husband, no friend now!' and immediately ran raving mad, and died in that state." Just as the intense love of Isaac Hayne's son for his father caused him to go mad and die after Hayne's execution, Mrs.Yarnall's affection for her husband, her "friend," drove her into madness and death.[160]

One woman's virtuous and exemplary devotion to her future husband made her a heroine of the war. Jane M'Crea was engaged to be married to a British officer. M'Crea remained in the Hudson Valley as

Burgoyne's troops pushed south toward Albany. A band of Wyandot Indians, whom the British were paying to collect rebel scalps, attacked the M'Crea homestead, and several Wyandots added M'Crea family scalps to their collection, including Jane's. In his schoolbook *History of the United States* (1822), William Grimshaw attributed the massacre to Indian greed.

> The engaging manners and beauty of this young lady having gained the heart of a British officer, he induced a return of her affection, and her consent to become his wife. Anxious for her safety, he wished to remove her from the neighbourhood of a hostile army. On the day appointed for the nuptials, he engaged a party of Indians to convey her to the camp; promising to reward the person who would accompany her, with a barrel of rum. Two of the Indians, both eager for the reward, disputed, after conveying her some distance, which should present her to the intended husband; and the one killed her with his tomahawk, to prevent the other from receiving it.[161]

Though the details of Grimshaw's account are wrong, the essential element of the story is correct. M'Crea's death was intimately related to her forthcoming marriage. The Indians, agents of the British, had prevented her from consummating her love. This fact alone made her more than just another victim of the war. She was a tragic figure because she had died as a result of her love for her fiancé. The circumstances of her death caught the imaginations of the American patriots, who gave M'Crea a special place in the iconography of the war's heroes and heroines.[162]

Whereas devotion to their husbands drew heroines from their homes into the war, the thoughts of heroes at war were drawn to home and wife. In one of the most dramatic anecdotes about an American war hero to appear in the early republic, David Humphreys described an ordeal Israel Putnam experienced early in Putnam's career. During a battle near Fort Edwards, Putnam was taken prisoner by an Indian, who tied the hero to a tree that stood between two warring camps. "Human imagination can hardly figure to itself a more deplorable situation," wrote Humphreys. "The balls flew incessantly from either side, many struck the tree, while some passed through the sleeves and skirts" of Putnam's coat. Putnam's "state of jeopardy" increased when an Indian happened upon him and decided to "excite the terrors of the prisoner, by hurling a tomahawk at his head . . . the weapon struck in the tree a number of times at a hair's breadth distance from the mark." Putnam's terror intensified when "a French Bas-Officer (a much more inveterate savage by nature, though descended from so humane and polished a nation) perceiving Putnam, came up to him, and, levelling a fuzzee within a foot of his breast attempted to discharge it; it missed fire. . . ." The climax of this ordeal came when Indians marched Putnam to their camp and "determined to roast him alive." They "stripped him naked, bound him to a tree and piled dry brush with other fuel, at a small distance in a circle round him." When they set the brush afire, "a sudden shower damped the rising flame." Again the Indians kindled the fire. Flames rose. The Indians "demonstrated the delerium of their joy by correspondent yells, dances and gesticulations." Putnam then "saw clearly that his final hour was inevitably come." In the face of death he "summoned all his resolution and composed his mind, as far as the circumstances could admit, to bid an eternal farewell to all he held most dear." Putnam would have died without "a single pang but for the idea of home, but for the remembrance of the affectionate partner of his soul, and of their beloved offspring." Fortunately, he lived to return to his wife and children. A French officer intervened at the last moment, smothering the flames that engulfed Putnam.[163]

Another hero of the war demonstrated a similar affection for wife and child. Joseph Warren's affection for his family was one of his key virtues. The *Analectic Magazine* observed in 1818 that he was "an example worthy of serious remembrance and imitation" because he combined the "most undaunted resolution in the field" with "the soft virtues of domestic life. . . ." An engraving for the *Columbian Magazine* is equivocal about Warren's "soft virtues" (fig. 30). The print shows Warren "taking leave of his wife and child on the eve of the battle of Bunker Hill." The hero stands, left arm raised as either a farewell or a gesture for his wife to desist from pleading with him to stay. Mrs. Warren looks with longing at her husband, clutches his gun, and points toward their child. There is an urgency in her posture that contrasts with her husband's firm stance and aloof gaze toward us, the spectators of this scene. Though the setting is domestic, providing evidence for Warren's attachment to his wife and child, the engraving reveals that Warren is willing to remove himself from them both psychologically and physically in order to defend his country. The print is a perfect visual expression of Benjamin Rush's contention that the republican citizen must "love his family, but . . . must . . . at the same time . . . forsake and even forget them when the welfare of his country requires it."[164]

Stories of Revolutionary heroes displaying extraordinary love for their fellow citizens are narrative expressions of more abstract Scottish Enlightenment ideas that, in part, provided a rationale for a shift from classical virtues requiring stoical fortitude to more achievable virtues rooted in sensibility. This transformation, which began in the mid-eighteenth century, continued into the early nineteen hundreds, preparing the way for the rise of both benevolent organizations and commerce.[165] Among portraits of heroes, there is perhaps no clearer single example of the new way of perceiving virtue than Weems' version of Francis Marion's meager dinner in the field with a British officer. Served a meal of potatoes only, the British officer speculates that Marion must "in general, no doubt, live a great deal better" than his current circumstances. When Marion replies that he in fact lives "rather worse," the British soldier wonders how Marion can stand such a life. "These things depend on feeling," explains Marion:

> The heart is all; and when that is much interested, a man can do anything. Many a youth would think it hard, to indent himself a slave for fourteen years.—But let him be over head and ears in love, and with such a beauteous sweetheart as Rachel, and he will think no more of fourteen year's servitude than young Jacob did. Well, now this is exactly my case. I am in love; and my love is LIBERTY.[166]

Weems' story replaces stoicism in the face of harsh wartime conditions with acceptance through love. Compared to Cato, the story of Marion and the British officer illustrates how much of the classical republican virtues Americans were leaving behind. The hero of Addison's play, written in 1755, faces death with equanimity because it is "earn'd by virtue." If not faced with death, Marion's reaction to hardship still reveals him forgoing Cato's stoical cerebral deliberation in favor of sentiment. The shift toward virtue based on sentiment served the needs of the new republic. According to the classical republicanism, virtue was formed by participation in the public life of the community. However, participation necessary to engender classical virtues seemed increasingly unavailable to most American citizens. Within twenty years of the war's end, biographers of its patriots began to offer portraits of heroes for "profit and improvement." Biography provided "the enterprising with a chart for their conduct." Instead of a means of emulating heroes, portraits of heroes now taught "every one to turn to the best account, the powers and means with which he is entrusted." In the preface to his compilation of the lives of great men, James Jones Wilmer explained how sentiment and profit were tied. It was essential, wrote Wilmer, for the reader to "minutely perceive the ideas, and enter into the feelings of the Author whose sentiments he professes to repeat. . . ." Mastering the art of reading this way was "an indispensible qualification, [for] particularly professional men, those who wish to attain eminence in the Senate, in the Pulpit, or at the Bar."[167]

Notions about the importance of affectionate relationships to republican government had an ideological role in justifying the Revolution. American colonists saw their relationship with Britain as a filial relationship gone awry. Britain was a parent to the colonies and, as such, merited the affection of Americans as long as she loved them. The mother country had demonstrated by her actions that she no longer did. Consequently, the colonists were not obligated to maintain their bond with her because a mother who "feels no love of species, but instead of it, entertains malice, rancour and ill will, we reckon totally immoral." As Weems wrote in his *Life of Washington*, the colonists "still loved her, and wished for nothing so much as . . . a glad return of all the former friendships and blessings." However, "*true friendship could never grow again where wounds of deadly hate had pierced so deep.*" Anecdotes that stressed the patriots' capacity for love and sympathetic feeling reminded readers that Americans had not been responsible for the breech of filial affection with Britain and suggested that they possessed sentiments necessary for virtue. More importantly, according to the prevailing belief in the power of example, these tales provided readers a means of sharpening their moral sense by sympathetically identifying with the Revolutionary heroes.[168]

THE PERSISTENCE OF CLASSICAL REPUBLICAN VIRTUES

In most biographies, magazines, and schoolbooks of the period, stories illustrating virtue based on sentiment were poor cousins to old ways of thinking about virtue. Portraits of Revolutionary heroes over-whelmingly stressed classical republican virtues—courage, patriotism, equanimity, benevolence, industriousness, piety, honesty, and humility.

Tales of sentiment appeared predominately in Weems' lives of Washington and Marion. Weems likely knew that southern readers were drawn to such stories in the way that many of the lower and middle class were attracted to evangelicalism. At the turn of the century, nearly thirty percent of the general southern population embraced evangelical Protestantism because it offered an attractive alternative to the prevailing ethos of competitiveness. In contrast to the inherent disorder, rivalry, and social distance of southern life, the evangelical community provided discipline, fellowship, and social intimacy. Discipline was essential to maintaining a way of life at odds with dominant southern manners and customs. Evangelicals rejected customs at the center of southern life; not only did they spurn the southerners' love of gambling, horse racing, and other more violent forms of competition, but they renounced genteel traditions like dancing. Surrounded by the heathenish practices of the non-converted, the evangelicals imposed a rigid discipline upon themselves to prevent lapses from their godly way of life. In place of the society they rejected, evangelicals formed a community based on fellowship and social intimacy. Social intimacy expressed itself by the ways evangelicals touched one another. Evangelicals often "prayed through personal crises with their arms around each other, and some greeted their brother and sisters in Christ with a kiss." Most intimate of all was the confession. A public declaration of one's sins, the confession was at the heart of the ritual by which men and women became members of the community. Yet, though the confession was a highly emotional, intimate experience, only the intensity of the confession was unique, for evangelicals commonly expressed emotions in ways that were unthinkable in traditional southern society.[169]

Weems portrayed a society strikingly similar to the evangelical community. In stories about Washington's childhood—the tale of the cherry tree, the story of the cabbage seeds, and the account of the lesson in the orchard—he described a world characterized by affection and friendship. Weems also stressed these qualities in anecdotes concerning Washington's adult life. Washington sorrowed for the victims of the French and Indian War and for starving livestock; and he offered Payne an apology in order to turn a rivalry into friendship. In his life of Marion, Weems created tales of affection with stories of Sergeant Jasper, Colonel Hayne, and Peter Yarnall. All in all, Weems' stories comprised a world that resembled the intimate, mutually supportive evangelical community. Like evangelicalism, Weems' stories may have appealed to middle class southern readers because they offered an attractive, if fictive, alternative to the harsh realities of everyday life.

Outside the South, biographers and authors of character sketches continued to emphasize classical republican virtues for ideological reasons. Federalists reacted to the Jeffersonian revolution and the burgeoning world of commerce by creating images of heroes that exemplified virtues the nation seemed to be leaving behind. Joseph Dennie offered readers of the *Port Folio* biographies of Anthony Wayne, Nicholas Biddle, Horatio Gates, Daniel Morgan, Philip Schuyler, and Henry Knox as lights in the "dark night of jacobinism," which, Dennie believed, had fallen on America in the first decade of the nineteenth century. Timothy Dwight and Edmund Randolph also wrote lives of heroes in reaction to changes in American life. In *Travels in New England and New York*, Dwight offered sketches of eminent men such as Israel Putnam and General Wadsworth to demonstrate that worthy individuals still remained as the center of a society threatened by economic and social change. Concern about unwelcome changes in the social and political condition of Virginia prompted Randolph to include a biography of Washington in his *History of Virginia*. The stress on classical virtues in schoolbooks also seems to have been in part a conservative reaction to changes in American life. In the late eighteenth and early nineteenth centuries, the schoolbook was largely a New England product. Most schoolbook authors were New England Federalists, and later, Whigs, who held that the future of the republic necessitated the Americans' adoption of classical virtues. To these men an educated, virtuous citizenry was crucial to the republic. They believed in the power of example and thought images of heroes could evoke the virtue necessary to assure the new nation's survival. The authors were outspoken advocates for reasserting classical virtues in the face of social, economic, and institutional change. To them, images of heroes were not merely expressions of nationalism, but ideological tools to shape the country's future generations.[170]

From 1780 through the early 1830s, printing and publishing decentralized from the cities to the rural areas of New England. Printers in towns such as Brookfield and Wrentham, Massachusetts; Fairhaven, Vermont; and Hallowell, Maine, turned out hundreds of new schoolbooks by Federalist authors. When overcrowding, soaring land prices, high taxes, and a desire for a more liberal religious and political atmosphere prompted large numbers of New Englanders to move west, printers of texts established shops along the frontier. The Picket brothers, for example, established a shop in Wheeling, West Virginia, where they wrote and printed schoolbooks for settlers of the Connecticut Western Reserve. Along the frontier, as well as in the Northeast, New Englanders produced school texts for New Englanders.[171]

New England women may have been the largest group of buyers of these texts. Before formal schooling, children often learned to read from their mothers at home. Benjamin Silliman, a prominent natural scientist of the mid-nineteenth century, reported to the *American Journal of Education* that "the elements of education were taught us by our mother at home along with religious instruction." Joseph Buckingham, editor of the *Polyanthos* and of the *Boston Daily Courier*, also reported that his mother used devotional material to teach him to read at home. Women taught reading outside the home as well. One of the most important ways city children acquired the rudimentary skills necessary to begin formal schooling was by attending dame schools run by neighborhood women. Moreover, as the common school movement grew in the early nineteenth century, increasing numbers of women attracted by prestige and economic incentives taught in schools and academies. Because local school boards had not yet assumed control of schoolbooks, mothers and schoolteachers, often women, chose the texts their children read.[172]

Women's involvement in education and schoolbook selection was part of their role as moral guardians of their children. Childhood was increasingly "seen as the training ground of individual virtue, and the mother . . . [was] its commander." J. S. C. Abbott observed in *The Mother at Home* (1833) that "Mothers have as powerful an influence over the welfare of future generations as all other earthly causes combined." This extraordinary influence occurred in the home, where women taught children the virtues of self-control, disinterested benevolence, and individual initiative. The Columbia College commencement address of 1795 asked that we "contemplate the mother [at home] distributing the mental nourishment to the fond smiling circle, by means proportionate to their different powers of reception, watching the gradual opening of their minds. . . . The Genius of Liberty hovers triumphant over the glorious scene. . . . Yes, ye fair, the reformation of a world is in your power. . . . Contemplate the rising glory of confederated America . . . Consider that your exertions can best secure, increase, and perpetuate it. . . . Liberty is never sure, 'till Virtue reigns triumphant. . . ." Women embraced these virtues as early nineteenth-century New England became increasingly industrialized. Self-control and individual initiative suited new forms of labor organization, especially those emerging in the textile mills, while a renewed emphasis on disinterested benevolence may have been a reaction to self-interest and self-alienation, byproducts of factory work. Moreover, following the Revolution, women were charged with forming the nation's republican citizens. Women were responsible for assuring that children would grow to be benevolent, industrious, pious, and, above all, patriotic men and women. Character sketches and anecdotes exemplifying classical republican virtues served the efforts of these New England women who taught the nation's youth to become responsible citizens.[173]

Apart from these articulated ideological agendas, classical republican virtues were intimately tied to an established biographical form—the recounting of historical events followed by a brief summation of virtues exemplified by a hero. Books written according to this convention portrayed a world in which communal history overshadowed private experience. While heroic public lives presupposed private virtue, the two were inseparable, the public life counting most. As much as conceptions of virtue were changing to accommodate the pursuit of individual gain during the period covered by this study, the traditional biographical form with its recitation of classical virtues changed slowly and haltingly. Weems' biographies of Washington illustrate the difficulty of melding new conceptions of virtue into the eighteenth-century biographical structure. On his first attempt at writing a life of Washington, Weems used a traditional approach to relate the hero's public achievements and praise those classical virtues that made such achievements possible. *A History, of the Life and Death, Virtues, and Exploits, of General George Washington* presented a chronological narrative of Washington's public life, interspersed with short anecdotes of Washington's public achievements. This early biography touted the time's standard view of exemplary history. Weems asserted that "of all the means tending to accomplish this *best* of ends [the teaching of virtue], there is none like that of setting before them the bright examples of persons eminent for their virtues." With the revision of 1808, Weems greatly increased the number of anecdotes, changing the biography from the chronicle/summation structure to a more fluid series of anecdotes. The formal change was more than incidental to Weems' new perception that "Private life is always *real life.*" Anecdotes replaced the customary historical chronicle because the recounting of public events could no longer reveal virtue with any certainty. Only in "the shade of private life" could one "see how soon, like a forced plant robbed of its hot-bed," the unauthentic hero "will drop his false foliage and fruit, and stand forth confessed in native stickweed sterility and worthlessness." The inclusion of anecdotes about private life, stories necessary both to reveal true virtue and to portray an exemplary life that the non-heroic reader might emulate, brought a change in the form of biography even though Weems continued to extol traditional virtues: temperance, equanimity, benevolence, piety, sincerity, and industry.[174]

THE ADVENT OF REALISM

Portraits of classical virtues went hand in hand with conventional eighteenth-century biographical forms in an overwhelming number of biographies, magazines, and schoolbooks of the early national period. Only a smattering of character sketches and biographies deviated from tradition by portraying flawed heroes. One such figure is Charles Lee, the misanthropic but brilliant general court-martialed after the Battle of Monmouth for disobeying Washington. Two magazines presented Lee as a misogynist rather than a model of virtue. Mathew Carey's *American Museum* recounted that "General Lee being one day surrounded, according to custom, by a numerous levee of his canine favorites, was asked by a lady, if he was fond of dogs? With his usual *politeness*, he instantly replied, 'Yes, madam, I love dogs; —but I detest bitches'."[175] The *Lancaster Hive* printed an anecdote about Lee that recalls the story of Washington and the ale cakes. The story tells how Lee, who was "remarkable slovenly in his dress and manners," entered a house where Washington was to meet him later. Lee

> went directly to the kitchen, and demanded something to eat; when
> the cook, taking him for a servant, told him she would give him
> victuals in a moment—but he must first help her off with the pot.
> This he complied with, and sat down to some cold meat which she
> placed for him on the dresser. The girl was remarkable inquisitive

about the guests who were coming, particularly of Lee, who she said she heard was one of the oddest and ugliest men in the world. In a few moments she desired the general again to assist her in placing on the pot, and scarce had he finished, when she requested him to take a bucket and go to the well. Lee made no objection, and began drawing the water.—In the mean time Gen. Washington arrived, and an aid-de-camp was dispatched in search of Lee: whom to his surprise, he found engaged as above—But what was the confusion of the poor girl, on hearing the aid-de-camp address the man with whom she had been so familiar, with the title of excellency!—The mug fell from her hand, and dropping on her knees, she began crying for pardon; when Lee, who was ever ready to see the impropriety of his own conduct, but never willing to change it, gave her a crown, and turning to the aid-de-camp, observed— "you see, young man, the advantage of a find [sic] coat—the man of consequence is indebted to it for respect; neither virtue nor abilities, without it, will make him look like a gentleman."[176]

Lee was, to be sure, a peripheral figure in the iconography of heroes of the Revolution; there were no other images during the fifty years following the war that presented a hero as lacking in classical virtues as these magazine sketches of Lee.

The portrait Weems drew of Francis Marion in his biography of the general was also out of step with prevailing images of heroes. The man that Weems described in his *Life of Marion* was "one little, swarthy, French-phizzed Carolinian" unlike any other Revolutionary figure to appear in early national biographies. Though Weems criticized Horatio Gates for being "rather too fond of his nocturnal glass," and lamented that many American officers' "laurels have been blasted by the flames of brandy," Marion himself seems to have suffered from excessive drinking on at least one occasion. "Dining with a squad of choice whigs, in Charleston, in the house of Mr. Alexander M'Queen, Tradd street, he was so frequently pressed to bumpers of old wine, that he found himself in a fair way to get drunk." After drinking an undisclosed number of bumpers of wine, Marion fell or jumped from the second story window of Mr. M'Queen's house. Weems' explanation of the mishap is ingenuous and amusing. Pressed to drink more, Marion "attempted to *beat a retreat*. The company swore that, *that would never do for general Marion.* Finding at last, that there was no other way of escaping *a debauch*, but by leaping out of one of the windows of the dining room, he bravely undertook it. It cost him, however, a broken ankle." According to Weems, God providently arranged the episode so that Marion would be away from Charleston when the British captured the city in 1780. Charleston "was invested with a large British army, and the American general (Lincoln), finding Marion was utterly unfit for duty, advised him to push off in a litter to his seat, in St. John's parish. Thus providentially was Marion preserved to his country when Charleston fell, as it soon did, with all our troops."[177]

In 1812, Weems had written *The Drunkard's Looking Glass*, a collection of anecdotes illustrating horrors of excessive drinking, especially of whiskey. To justify Marion's drunkenness as providential illustrates Weems' tendency to manipulate material to suit his needs, a trait nearly all the parson's critics have commented on. Behavior that Weems presented as deplorable in the tract is, in *Life of Marion*, part of God's plan. In his attempt to fashion a romance out of Marion's war adventures, Weems could hardly use the incident at M'Queen's to rail against the dangers of drinking. To do so would undermine the stature of his hero; instead, Weems allows Marion himself to speak of the evils of alcohol later in the biography.[178]

However much Weems succeeded in making Marion's broken ankle a product of the hero's virtue and God's providence, the inclusion in the biography of this story was a subtle yet important difference from other anecdotes about heroes of the Revolution. During the fifty years following the war, no other story puts a hero in such a position of compromise requiring a special explanation to exonerate him. There is in this story of Marion's fall from M'Queen's second-story window a touch of forthright realism that is unmatched in other biographical portraits of Revolutionary heroes, including Weems' earlier portrait of Washington.

This realism manifests itself also in Marion's relationship with his soldiers. Marion leads them with some difficulty, and his stature as a hero is often established by lectures on virtue rather than virtuous action itself. Sometimes the lectures are post-mortem reflections on near disasters. In one instance, several of Marion's officers loot a house occupied by the wife and children of an American Tory. Among the prizes taken is a sword. Outraged, Marion demands its return to the Tory's wife. A threat of mutiny arises when Marion makes the demand, and dissipates only when he calls for a file of soldiers to shoot the officer holding the sword. After the incident, Marion delivers a speech on the "*commonwealth of brothers* . . . where men, reaping as they sow, feel the utmost stimulus to every virtue that can exalt the human character and condition!" The hero concludes by telling his men,

> Our enemies are blind. They neither *understand* nor *desire the happiness of mankind*. Ignorant, therefore, as children, they claim our pity: our pity for *themselves*. And as to their widows and little ones, the very thought of *them* should fill our souls with tenderness. The crib that contains their corn, the cow that gives them milk, the cabin that shelters their feeble heads from the storm, should be sacred in our eyes.[179]

This is a Weemsian homily. Whereas the parson frequently digressed in *Life of Washington* to lecture about the meaning of his anecdotes or the importance of Washington's virtues, in *Life of Marion* he gave the lectures to the hero himself. In the case of the homily following the looting and near mutiny, the parson commented on the value of the Marion/Weems speech, claiming that the satisfaction it "gave to the officers was so general and sincere, that I often heard them say afterwards, that, since the mutiny was suppressed, they were glad it had happened; for it had given them an opportunity to hear a lecture, which they hoped would make them better men and braver soldiers too, as long as they lived."[180]

Later, Marion's men revolt once more, and the hero again turns the disaster into an opportunity to lecture. In this anecdote, the revolt takes place during a scouting mission by men commanded by Captain Clarke and Peter Horry, the alleged author of the biography and source of many of Weems' stories about Marion. Captain Clarke and several men happened upon the British who, "sounding their bugles . . . rushed on to the charge. Unfortunately, Clarke had not seen the enemy, and mistaking their bugles for the huntsmen's horns, ordered a halt to see the deer go by." Upon discovering that the deer were British soldiers, Marion's troops "themselves metamorphosed into deer" and high-tailed it, despite repeated commands to halt and fight. When Marion hears about this incident, his response is entirely pragmatic. He tells Horry not to expect much of the militia. "If, on turning out against the enemy, you find your men in high spirits with burning eyes all kindling around you, then's your time; then in close columns, with sounding bugles and shining swords dash on . . . But, on the other hand, if by any unlooked for providence they get dismayed, and begin to run . . . you must learn to run too: and as fast as they; nay, *faster*, that you may get into the front, and encourage them to rally."[181]

The realism that recurs in *Life of Marion* gave rise to some unusually frank scenes involving other characters. One is the death of Sergeant Jasper. Jasper's last moments conform to neoclassical standards of decorum regarding death, with the exception of the very last moment. At that time, the hero, wrote Weems, made a "feeble effort to vomit," and convulsed before he died. Unpleasant physiological details were not part of the conventions that governed the description of heroes' deaths. In another instance, Weems repeated a story he first read in a Charleston newspaper about a Mr. Smith, who was arrested for being a Tory and was handcuffed to another prisoner. Together the two prisoners escaped, running through the countryside until the "poor sickly creature of a tory" to whom Mr. Smith was bound, collapsed.

> Confined by the handcuffs, Smith was obliged to lie by him in the woods, two days and nights without drink! and his comrade frequently in convulsions! on the third day he died. Unable to bear it any longer Smith drew his knife and separated himself from the dead man, by cutting off his arm at the elbow, which he bore with him to Charleston.[182]

As with the story of Sergeant Jasper's death, the gruesome details of this story were highly unusual occurrences in a biography of the early national period.

In addition to making the biography uncommonly realistic, Weems filled it with an unprecedented diversity of minor heroes, a practice that James Fenimore Cooper would develop in his early novel, *The Spy* (1821). Weems' minor heroes include a black, a British commander, and several ladies of North Carolina. The first of these was Cudjo, black overseer of a Carolinian named Snipes whose home was attacked by Tories. Cudjo helped Snipes escape, but was captured himself. After failing to force the overseer to reveal his master's hiding place, the Tories clapped a halter round his neck, and told him to get "down on his knees, and say his prayers at once, for he had but two minutes to live!"

He replied, that he "did not want to say his prayers *now*, for that he was no *thief*, and had always been a true slave to his master."

This fine sentiment of the poor black was entirely lost on our *malignant whites* who throwing the end of the halter over the limb of an oak, tucked him up as though he had been a mad dog. He hung till he was nearly dead; when one of them called out: "d——n him, cut him down. I'll be bound he'll tell us now." Cudjo was, accordingly, cut down; and, as soon as a little recovered, questioned again about his master. But he still declared he knew nothing of him. He was then hoisted a second time; and a second time, when nearly dead, cut down and questioned as before: but still he asserted his ignorance. The same inhumane part was acted on him a *third time*, but with no better success: for the brave fellow still continued faithful to his master, who, squatted and trembling in his place of torment, his briar bush, saw and heard all that was passing.

Persuaded now that Cudjo really knew nothing of his master, they gave up the shameful contest, and went off; leaving him half dead on the ground, but covered with glory.[183]

This horrid Tory atrocity is tempered by the anecdote that immediately follows it. The second anecdote tells of a British Major Muckleworth who, in a generous and humanitarian spirit, dispatches a surgeon to care for Marion's wounded troops and offers to pay a widow for the use of her house as a hospital. The widow refuses the money, saying that she "was all *one as his prisoner*," and, therefore, need not be paid. Echoing Marion's speech to his mutinous troops, Muckleworth declares, "My king, . . . Madam does not make war against widows . . . the word of God assures us, that his ear is always open to the cry of the widow and orphan: and believe me, madam, I dread their cry more than I do the shouts of an enemy's army."[184]

The similarity between Marion's speech to his troops and Muckleworth's comments to the widow suggest that here again Weems is delivering one of his homilies. Yet, that Weems would use a British commander as his spokesman is unusual. Most British throughout the biography are like Major Wemyss, who "no more regarded the sacred cries of angel-watched children than the Indians do the cries of young beavers, whose houses they are breaking up." Weems repeatedly contrasted the "savage spirit" of Wemyss and other British soldiers to the concern American heroes showed towards the war's victims.[185]

One instance of this concern occurred when Marion and his troops attacked a house the British had converted into a fort. After a prolonged, unsuccessful fight, Marion determined he could drive the British from the house only by setting it on fire. However, the general hesitated as he thought of the effect this action might have on the woman (yet another widow) who owned the property. "But poor Mrs. Motte! a lone widow, whose plantation had been so long ravaged by the war, herself turned into a log cabin, her negroes dispersed, and her stock, grain, &c. nearly all ruined! must she now loose her elegant buildings too?" Marion was spared the dilemma his concern for the widow created by the heroic Mrs. Motte herself.

> For at the first glimpse of the proposition, she exclaimed, "O! burn it! burn it, general Marion! God forbid I should bestow a single thought on my little concerns, when the independence of my country is at stake. No, sir, if it were a palace it should go." Then she stepped to her closet and brought out a curious bow with a quiver of arrows, which a poor African boy purchased from on board a Guineamen, had formerly presented her, and said, "here, general, here is what will serve your purpose to a hair." The arrows, pointed with iron, and charged with lighted combustibles, were shot on the top of the house, to which they stuck and quickly communicated the flames. The British, two hundred in number, besides a good many tories, instantly hung out a white flag, in sign of submission.
>
> The excellent Mrs. Motte was present when her fine new house, supposed to be worth six thousand dollars, took fire; and, without a sigh, beheld the red spiry billows prevailing over all its grandeur.[186]

Mrs. Motte's patriotism was shared by other women of North Carolina. According to Weems, there was a common "female detestation of the British. . . ." The women openly scorned the British "and in short, turned away from them as from the commonest felons or cutthroats . . . to be treated thus by *buckskin girls*, the *rebel* daughters of *convict* parents, was more than the British officers could put up with."[187]

With changes in Weems' portrayal of a Revolutionary general and the minor heroes about him, came a change in form and style. Weems based the *Life of Marion* on documents given to him by Peter Horry, a soldier who had served under the general. Horry wanted Weems to write a biography in the style of the parson's immensely successful *Life of Washington*; that is, Horry looked forward to an account of Marion's early years, his public career, and his great virtues. Weems had something else in mind. He wrote Horry in December, 1809, "You have no doubt constantly kept in memory, *that I told you I must write it in my own way, and knowing the passion of the times for novels, I have endeavoured to throw your facts and ideas about Gen. Marion into the garb and dress of a military romance.*" Just as Weems' understanding of the demands of readers had shaped his biography of Washington, his sense of Americans' passion for novels led him to put "*facts and ideas about Gen. Marion into the garb and dress of a military romance.*" The result, much to Horry's displeasure, was a hodgepodge of style and form.[188]

Weems began with an eye on his stated intention to write a romance. Chapter 1, a "*SHORT sketch of an extraordinary French couple, viz. the grandfather and mother of our hero,*" tells how Gabriel Marion and his new bride, Louisa, were expelled from France. According to Weems' account, officers of the Inquisition informed Marion, a Huguenot, that his "damnable heresy well deserve[d] . . . purgation by fire," but they would spare his life if he would leave France within ten days. The ultimatum terrified grandfather Marion, but his greatest fear was of losing his wife. "How could he hope she would consent to leave her parents and friends to wander and die with him in hopeless exile?" His fears were quickly dispelled, however, when Louisa begged him to

> give me your company, my Gabriel, and then welcome that foreign land with all its shady forests! Welcome the thatched cottage and the little garden filled with the fruits of our own fondly mingled toils! Methinks, my love, I already see that distant sun rising with gladsome beams on our dew spangled flowers. I hear the wild wood-birds pouring their sprightly carols on the sweet scented morning. My heart leaps with joy for their songs.[189]

Writing in comically florid prose, Weems worked the romance formula in which a wife decorates a "summer house with evergreens and flowers of the liveliest tints" to receive her husband, and lovers sigh to part. Nonetheless, the parson did not adhere for long to the romance form. After the first chapter of the biography, he reverted to the conventional biographical structure, narrating the hero's public life (only two pages tell of Marion's childhood and youth) and concluding with a summary of his character traits.

Perhaps Weems' efforts to write a romance of Marion's life caused him to experiment with the different voices that one finds in the biography. Sometimes he has a character speak in language so mannered that it collapses in parody, as when Horry exclaims,

> Oh Marion, my friend! my friend! never can I forget thee. Although thy wars are all ended, and thyself at rest in the grave, yet I see thee still. I see thee as thou wert wont to ride, most terrible in battle to the enemies of thy country. Thine eyes, like balls of fire, flamed beneath thy lowering brows. But lovely still wert thou in mercy. . . . The basest tory who could but touch the hem of thy garment was safe. The avengers of blood stopped short in thy presence, and turned away abashed from the lightning of thine eyes.[190]

If Weems' attempt to write lofty prose for lofty occasions fails, his efforts to create humorous dialogue are hardly more successful. What is of interest in them is his use of dialect. For instance, Weems presents *in medias res* an exchange between Count D'Estang and Henry Laurens, interpreter between the Count and General Lincoln:

> "But monsieur le count," said Lauren to D'Estang, "the American officers say they are afraid you have given the English too long time to think."
>
> . . . The count put on a most *comic* stare, and breaking into a hearty laugh, replied, "de Engleesh tink! hal ha! ha!—By gar dat vun ver good parole! De Engleesh tink, heh, monsieur le colonel! By gar, de Engleesh never tink but for *deir bellie.* Give de Jack Engleeshman plenty beef—plenty pudding—plenty porter, by gar he never tink any more, he lay down, he go sleep like von hog."[191]

Weems' use of dialect is not new to *Life of Marion*. In the Washington biography, Weems attempted to write black dialect when he told the story of another Cudjo, a pilot who was sounding for the depth of water. The ship's captain asked Cudjo, *"'what water have you got there?' 'What water, massa? what water? why salt water, to be sure, sir.'"* Again, dialect occurs when Weems attempts humor. Although attempts at humor through dialect occur in *Life of Washington*, they appear more frequently in the later biography.[192]

Weems' *Life of Marion* continued his movement away from conventional eighteenth-century biography. That movement began with the parson's biography of Washington. In the first edition of 1800 and its revision of 1808, Weems used the standard biographical structure of the day, but modified its shape as he included anecdotes about Washington's childhood and wartime experiences. Unlike his approach to *Life of Washington*, Weems' purpose in writing the biography of Marion was to create a romance, something quite different from the biographies of heroes being written in early nineteenth-century America. Though Weems did not succeed, *Life of Marion* was written with a greater realism than any other biography of the time, creating a character unlike the typical unvaryingly virtuous Revolutionary hero. The biography also included an unusual number of heroes other than Marion. In structure and style the biography was distinctive, as Weems cast part of it into the mold of the romance and attempted to vary his style to fit various occasions.

Magazines and schoolbooks rarely offered sketches of Revolutionary patriots that diverged from the traditional portrait of the exemplary hero. Among magazines, there was only the picturesque figure of Charles Lee. *Practical Reading Lessons*, a school reader published in 1830, offered several anecdotes about minor heroes of the Revolution. Among these were Weems' story about Mrs. Motte. Another story of "female heroism" related how "Mrs. S. of Carolina" held at bay British soldiers pursuing an American rebel who hid in her bedroom by saying, "to men of honour, the chamber of a lady should be as sacred as a sanctuary. I will defend mine, though I perish." According to the schoolbook lesson, Mrs. S.'s speech was enough to dissuade the British from opening the bedroom door. *Practical Reading Lessons* also told of an unknown American soldier who did not cry out when a British doctor amputated his arm because "he would not have breathed a sigh, in the presence of British officers, to have secured a long and fortunate existence." Other stories of courage and patriotism illustrated virtues the author of the schoolbook wished his pupils to adopt. Yet, *Practical Reading Lessons* was unique in the attention it gave to previously unsung heroes and heroines of the Revolution. Two other texts published around 1830 were unusual for the attention they devoted to recounting the life of Washington. In 1829, the American Sunday School Union published Anna Reed's *Life of Washington*. Reed's biography was an inspirational tract meant to elicit among children the "delightful assurance, that we are always under the watchful care of our powerful and kind Creator." Reed recounted Washington's history, including in her narration an occasional anecdote, such as Weems' story of Washington praying at Valley Forge. She hoped when children had finished the biography they would see that "Through all his toilsome and tempting course, [Washington] was true, just, industrious, temperate, honest, generous, brave, human, modest—a real lover of his country, and a humble worshipper of God." Likewise, Samuel Goodrich, the putative author of another school biography of Washington, recounted the hero's public life and repeated the well-known list of Washington's character traits and virtues. *Practical Reading Lessons*, Reed's Sunday school book, and Goodrich's biography, abandoning the short rhetorical lesson typical of the period's readers, offered children extended accounts of Washington's life. Still, despite these intimations of change, continuity characterized images of heroes during the fifty years following the American Revolution. From David Humphreys' portrait of Israel Putnam to Samuel Goodrich's life of George Washington, images presented the Revolutionary hero as an embodiment of the nation's history and a model of virtue. By reading about the heroes' lives, Americans could form their own virtuous behavior. This would change in the next decade. The historical romance and the biography of private life would displace exemplary biography. A new conception of the hero and heroism would emerge too as the adventures and rugged individualism of Daniel Boone and Andrew Jackson captured the imagination of Americans.[193]

Notes

1. Rosemarie Zagarri, introduction to *"Life of General Washington" with George Washington's "Remarks,"* by David Humphreys, ed. Rosemarie Zagarri (Athens, GA: Univ. of Georgia Press, 1991), xx-xxi; Jedidiah Morse, *The American Geography; or, a View of the Present Situation of the United States of America* (Elizabethtown: Shepard Kollock, 1789), 127–32; Morse, *The Life of General Washington, Commander in Chief . . . and Present President* (Philadelphia: Jones, Hoff, Derrick, 1794). The Humphrey/Morse sketch appeared in Morse's *Prayer and Sermon at Charlestown . . . on the Death of George Washington . . . with an Additional Sketch of His Life* (Charlestown: Samuel Etheridge, 1800); *The Washingtoniana: Containing a Biographical Sketch of the Late Gen. George Washington, with Various Outlines of His Character, . . .* (Baltimore: Samuel Sower, 1800); and *Memory of Washington: Comprising a Sketch of His Life and Character; and the National Testimonials of Respect . . .* (Newport, RI: Oliver Farnsworth, 1800).

2. William Spohn Baker, *Bibliotheca Washingtoniana. A Descriptive List of the Biographies and Biographical Sketches of George Washington* (Philadelphia: Robert M. Lindsay, 1889); *Washington's Political Legacies. To Which is Annexed an Appendix, Containing an Account of his Illness, Death, and the National Tributes of Respect Paid to his Memory, with a Biographical Outline of His Life and Character* (Boston: n.p., 1800), reprinted in Trenton, New Jersey, as *Legacies of Washington: Being a Collection of the Most Approved Writings of the Late General Washington, with an Appendix, Containing a Sketch of the Life of this Illustrious Patriot* (Trenton: Sherman, Mershon, and Thomas, 1800); Thomas Condie, *Biographical Memoirs, of the Illustrious Gen. George Washington, late President of the United States of America, etc. etc. Containing A History of the Principal Events of his Life, with*

Extracts from his Journals, Speeches to Congress, and Public Addresses. Also, a Sketch of his Private Life (Philadelphia: Charless and Ralston, 1800). I discuss the magazine sketch in chapter 2. William Allen, *An American Biographical and Historical Dictionary: Containing an Account of the Lives, Characters, and Writings of the Most Eminent Persons in North America from Its First Discovery to the Present Time, and a Summary of the History of the Several Colonies and of the United States* (Cambridge, MA: Hilliard and Metcalf, 1809); John Kingston, *The New American Biographical Dictionary; or, Memoirs of Many of the Most Eminent Persons that Have Ever Lived in This or Any Other Nation* . . . (Baltimore: n.p., 1810); Joseph Delaplaine, *Delaplaine's Repository of the Lives and Portraits of Distinguished Americans* (Philadelphia: William Brown, 1817–18), 1:105–6; Thomas Wilson, *Biography of Principle Military and Naval Heroes Comprehending Details of Their Achievements during the Revolutionary and Late Wars*, 2 vols. (New York: John Low, 1817–19); Thomas Woodward, *The Columbian Plutarch; or an Exemplification of Several Distinguished Characters* (Philadelphia: Clark and Raser, 1819).

3. *Washington's Political Legacies*, 115–16.

4. In a letter to the publisher of Marshall's multi-volume *Life of George Washington*, Mason Locke Weems wrote that "people like a stout penny's worth for their penny." Wayne had printed the second edition of the biography on thin paper, prompting Weems to note that the size of the volumes had halved. Weems feared that buyers would "raise a talk, a hue and a cry" at the price, which remained at six dollars per volume. Weems to C. P. Wayne, January 25, 1805, *Mason Locke Weems: His Works and His Ways*, ed. Emily Ellsworth Ford Skeel (New York: n.p., 1929), 2:311. By comparison, novels of the period cost between $.75 and $1.50. Cathy N. Davidson, *Revolution and the Word: The Rise of the Novel in America* (New York: Oxford Univ. Press, 1986), 25.

5. Davidson, 25.

6. William Johnson, *Sketches of the Life and Correspondence of Nathaneal Greene, Major General of the Armies of the United States, in the War of the Revolution* (Charleston: A. E. Miller, 1822), 1:viii; John Marshall, *Life of George Washington* (Philadelphia: C. P. Wayne, 1804–8), 1:xi; John Henry Sherburne, *Life and Character of Chevalier John Paul Jones* (Washington: n.p., 1825); David Humphreys, *An Essay on the Life of the Honorable Major-General Israel Putnam* (Hartford: n.p., 1788); William Dobein James, *A Sketch of the Life of Brig. Gen. Francis Marion* (Charleston: Gould and Riley, 1821); Charles Caldwell, *Memoirs of the Life and Campaigns*

of the Hon. Nathaniel Greene, Major General in the Army of the United States (Philadelphia: n.p., 1819); Aaron Bancroft, *An Essay on the Life of George Washington* (Worcester: Thomas and Sturvent, 1807); David Ramsay, *The Life of George Washington* (New York: n.p., 1807); Jonathan Clark, *Life of General Washington* (Albany: Packard and Benthuysen, 1813).

7. Meyer Reinhold, *The Classick Pages: Classical Reading of Eighteenth-Century Americans* (University Park, PA: The American Philological Association, 1975), 39–47; George H. Nadel, "Philosophy of History Before Historicism," *History and Theory* 3 (1964), 298; Henry St. John, Lord Viscount Bolingbroke, "Letters on the Study and Use of History," *Works* (London: J. Johnson et al., 1809), 3:306–12.

8. Bolingbroke, "Letters on the Study and Use of History," 3:334–35, 3:325–26; H. T. Dickinson, *Bolingbroke* (London: Constable & Co., Ltd., 1970), 250–51; Simon Varey, *Henry St. John, Viscount Bolingbroke* (Boston: Twayne Publishers, 1984), 78–81.

9. *Pennsylvania Packet,* January 28, 1779; Samuel S. Smith to James Madison, November 1777–August 1778, *Papers,* ed. William T. Hutchinson and William M. E. Rachal (Chicago: Univ. of Chicago Press, 1962), 1:208. An uncommon dissent from this enthusiasm for Bolingbroke's theory came from John Adams, who believed that "Images of fools and knaves are as easily made as those of patriots and heroes . . . the fine arts . . . promote virtue while virtue is in fashion." Quoted in Neil Harris, *The Artist in American Society: The Formative Years 1790–1860* (New York: George Braziller, 1966), 36.

10. Book buyers were apparently put off by Marshall's broad history. Weems told C. P. Wayne, "*General Marshall told me* that both Himself and Judge Washington were decidedly of opinion, that the 1st Vol, having not a word about Washington in it, shd not appear with the 2d. . . ." Weems to C. P. Wayne, February 15, 1804, 2:293. Lester H. Cohen provides a study of exemplary history in *The Revolutionary Histories: Contemporary Narratives of the American Revolution* (Ithaca: Cornell Univ. Press, 1980); Marshall, *Life of George Washington,* 5:773.

11. Marshall, *Life of George Washington,* 5:774; John Adams to Thomas Jefferson, July 13, 1813, *The Adams-Jefferson Letters,* ed. Lester J. Cappon (Chapel Hill: Univ. of North Carolina Press, 1959), 2:349. Cohen, surveying characterizations of Washington by historians of the period, argues that Washington "embodies both the characteristics of the 'leader' and of the 'typical hero of romance,' to use [Northrup] Frye's term." *The Revolutionary Histories,* 226–27.

12. Donald A. Stauffer, *The Art of Biography in Eighteenth Century England* (Princeton: Princeton Univ. Press, 1941), 519–20.

13. Weems to C. P. Wayne, April 8, 1803, 2:264–65.

14. Joseph F. Kett and Patricia A. McClung, "Book Culture in Post-Revolutionary Virginia," *Proceedings of the American Antiquarian Society,* 94 (1984), 119–38; Weems to Carey, August 9, 1800, 2:136. Ronald J. Zboray discusses Weems' attempts to tailor books to his market, including bowdlerizing books such as Paine's *Age of Reason,* and notes that Weems pitched to the segment of society that bought books, the gentry. *A Fictive People: Antebellum Economic Development and the American Reading Public* (New York: Oxford Univ. Press, 1993), 50–51. Weems to Carey, July 29, 1798, 2:105; ibid., September 16, 1796, 2:34; ibid., December 18, 1809, 2:428; ibid., March 25, 1809, 2:397.

15. Weems to Carey, March 8, 1811, 3:39; ibid., December 18, 1811, 3:58; ibid., March 27, 1809, 2:400; ibid., October 30, 1797, 2:91.

16. James Gilreath, "Mason Locke Weems, Mathew Carey, and the Southern Booktrade, 1794–1810," *Publishing History* 10 (1981), 27–50; Weems to Carey, March 10, 1798, 2:97–99; ibid., March 25, 1809, 2:397; ibid., January 22, 1797, 2:72.

17. Weems to Carey, January 22, 1797, 2:72; ibid., January 12 or 13, 1800, 2:127–28; ibid., February 2, 1800, 2:127.

18. Mason Locke Weems, *A History, of the Life and Death, Virtues, and Exploits, of General George Washington . . . Happily calculated to Furnish a Feast of True Washingtonian Entertainment and Improvement, Both to Ourselves and our Children* (Georgetown: Green & English, 1800), 3; ibid., preface.

19. Weems, *History of General George Washington,* 7.

20. Ibid., 8.

21. Ibid., 25.

22. Ibid., 31, 46, 78, 79.

23. Ibid., 38–39.

24. Quoted in Douglas Southall Freeman, *George Washington, A Biography* (New York: Charles Scribner's Sons, Inc., 1954), 2:146–47; Weems, *History of General George Washington,* 39.

25. Freeman, *George Washington,* 2:146.

26. Weems, *History of General George Washington,* 38; Rhys Isaac, *The Transformation of Virginia, 1740–1790* (Chapel Hill: Univ. of North Carolina Press, 1982), 81, 85; Weems, *History of General George Washington,* 40.

27. Isaac, *Transformation of Virginia,* 99.

28. Richard R. Beeman, ed. "Trade and Travel in Post-Revolutionary Virginia: A Diary of an Itinerant Peddler, 1807–1808," *The Virginia Magazine of History and Biography* 84 (1976), 183; C. C. Pearson and J. Edwin Hendricks, *Liquor and Anti-Liquor in Virginia, 1619–1919* (Durham, NC: Duke Univ. Press, 1967), 113; W. J. Rorabaugh, *The Alcoholic Republic: An American Tradition* (New York: Oxford Univ. Press, 1979), 27–28; Isaac, *Transformation of Virginia*, 95; Isaac Weld, Jr., *Travels Through the States of North America,* 2 vols. (London: John Stockdale, 1799), 1:191–92; quoted in Weld, *Travels,* 1:98.

29. Bertram Wyatt-Brown, *Southern Honor: Ethics & Behavior in the Old South* (New York: Oxford Univ. Press, 1982), 338; quoted by Isaac, *Transformation of Virginia,* 319.

30. Mason Locke Weems, *The Life of George Washington: With Curious Anecdotes, Equally Honorable to Himself, and Exemplary to his Young Countrymen,* 6th ed. (Philadelphia: R. Cochran, 1808), 11; ibid., 21.

31. Isaac, *Transformation of Virginia,* 122; Kett and McClung, "Book Culture," 136–37; Isaac, *Transformation of Virginia,* 122–23; Wyatt-Brown, *Southern Honor,* 47.

32. Weems, *The Life of George Washington,* 4; ibid., 4.

33. Samuel Johnson, *The Rambler,* vol. 3 of *The Yale Edition of the Works of Samuel Johnson,* ed. W. J. Bate and Albrecht B. Strauss (New Haven and London: Yale Univ. Press, 1969), 321. William A. Bryan, while noting that Weems' comments are Johnsonian, does not believe Weems to have necessarily had Johnson in mind when writing the new introductory passage. "The Genesis of Weems's 'Life of Washington'," *Americana* 36 (1942), 149. Still, Johnson's *Rambler* essay and Weems' comments are remarkably similar. Weems sold Johnson's essays and may have been familiar with the Englishman's views on biography.

34. Emily Ellsworth Ford Skeel writes that "at the age of nineteen Mason received one negro boy, the reversion, in case of his elder brother's death, of Paschales Purchase, and a third share of the residuary estate, which probably included at least one slave. He evidently emancipated them very quickly. . . ." Skeel, *Works and Ways,* 3:389; Weems to Carey, June 19, 1807, 2:364.

35. Weems, *The Life of George Washington,* 6; Johnson, *The Rambler,* 320.

36. Weems, *The Life of George Washington,* 11.

37. Ibid., 1314.

38. For a discussion of contemporary reactions to the story, see Gary Wills, "Mason Weems, Bibliopolist," *American Heritage* 32 (1981), 67–68; Clark, *Life of General Washington*, 9.

39. Marcus Cunliffe, introduction to *The Life of Washington, by Mason Locke Weems*. Ed. Marcus Cunliffe (Cambridge, MA: Harvard Univ. Press, 1962), xxxii; quoted by Cunliffe, "Introduction," xxxii.

40. Weems, *The Life of George Washington*, 16.

41. Gary Wills argues that Mr. Washington's education-by-example was intended to prepare George for public life by molding him into a Cincinnatus figure. *Cincinnatus: George Washington and the Enlightenment* (Garden City, NY: Doubleday and Company, Inc., 1984), 49–53.

42. Jay Fliegelman makes the analogy to the fortunate fall in *Prodigals and Pilgrims: The American Revolution Against Patriarchal Authority, 1750–1800* (Cambridge: Cambridge Univ. Press, 1982), 202; Weems, *The Life of George Washington,* 20.

43. Weems, *The Life of George Washington*, 21.

44. Ibid., 87.

45. Weems to Carey, December 17, 1800, 2:157; ibid., October 18, 1805, 2:329; ibid., March 19, 1799, 2:114.

46. The geographical distribution of magazines offering portraits coincides with Frank Luther Mott's observations on the rise of magazines. See Frank Luther Mott, *A History of American Magazines, 1741–1850*, vol. 1 of *A History of American Magazines, 1741–1930* (New York: D. Appleton and Company, 1930), 31–33, 204–8.

47. Edward M. Cifelli, *David Humphreys* (Boston: Twayne Publishers, 1982), 15–18, 74–76.

48. *Monthly Anthology* 9 (1810), 414–19; *Blackwood's Magazine* 17 (1825), 203.

49. Benjamin T. Spencer, *The Quest for Nationality: An American Literary Campaign* (Syracuse: Syracuse Univ. Press, 1957), 26.

50. Quoted in John Allen Krout and Dixon Ryan Fox, *The Completion of Independence, 1790–1830* (New York: The Macmillan Company, 1944), 209; Alex De Tocqueville, *Democracy in America,* trans. Henry Reeve (New York: The Century Co., 1898), 1:311.

51. Morse, *The American Geography*, 127–32. The sketch was later reprinted, along with a sketch of Richard Montgomery, in *The Life of General Washington, Commander in Chief . . . and Present President* (Philadelphia: Jones, Hoff and Derrick, 1794). Zagarri, "Introduction," xxi; *The Massachusetts Magazine* 1 (1789), 289–90; Skeel, *Works and Ways,* 1:4.

Lavater's treatise was published in England in 1789: *Essays on Physiognomy,* trans. by T. Holcroft, 3 vols. (London, 1789). An American edition was issued in 1794.

An annotation in the Boston Atheneum's copy of *The Columbian Magazine* suggests that the profile may be of Silas Dean. In the copy she examined at the Library Company of Philadelphia, Wick found an annotation next to the illustration stating the Franklin profile was "very like him" but the Washington "is little like Him." Wendy C. Wick, *George Washington, An American Icon: The Eighteenth-Century Graphic Portraits* (Washington, D.C.: Smithsonian Institution Traveling Exhibition Service, 1982), 98. In the early republic, images purporting to be likenesses of Washington were frequent enough to cause the American Academy of Fine Arts to issue "Remarks of General Washington" in 1824. The report lamented that "we are cursed as a nation with the common, miserable representations of our Great Hero, and with the shocking counterfeits of his likeness by every pitiful bungler that lifts a tool or a brush, working solely from imagination without any authority for their representations and deceptions, and bolstered up by every kind of imposture." The Academy certified six portraits as authentic for various needs. "Academy of Fine Arts: Remarks on Portraits of General Washington, 1824," in John W. McCoubrey, ed., *American Art, 1700–1960: Sources and Documents* (Englewood Cliffs, NJ: Prentice-Hall, Inc., 1965), 26–27. For another example of this practice, see my remarks in chapter 3 on illustrations in the schoolbook *History of America* (1795). *The Columbian Magazine* 2 (1788), 145. The engraving is catalogued in Charles Henry Hart, *Catalogue of the Engraved Portraits of Washington* (New York: The Grolier Club, 1904), no. 810; Wick, *American Icon*, no. 23; and Donald H. Cresswell, comp., *The American Revolution in Drawings and Prints: A Checklist of 1765–1790 Graphics in the Library of Congress* (Washington, DC: Library of Congress, 1975), no. 225. In the last of four volumes of a 1797 edition of the treatise, Lavater declared, "I mistrust the accuracy of resemblance in all engraved portraits, and I believe I have said before, that, in general, I look upon the representations of celebrated men, as so many caricatures." The remark, which introduced another attempt to read Washington's character from a graphic portrait, is ironic, for the portrait is fictitious.

52. *The Massachusetts Magazine* 3 (1791), 139–143.

53. *The Port Folio* 5 (1806), 187; *The Literary Miscellany* 2 (1806), 118–19; *The Port Folio* 5 (1808), 187–89; *The Literary Miscellany* 2 (1806), 118–19; *The Literary Miscellany* 1 (1811), 3–13.

54. Weems to Carey, March 15, 1809, 2:395. On the popularity of Washington's portrait, see also Wick, *American Icon.*

Hart, *Engraved Portraits of Washington*, no. 143; Wick, *American Icon*, no. 28; *Dictionary of American Biography*, vol. 20, 559. The engraving is listed also in W. S. Baker, *The Engraved Portraits of Washington* (Philadelphia: Lindsay and Baker, 1880), no. 77. *The Philadelphia Monthly Magazine, or Universal Repository* 1 (1798) (Hart, *Engraved Portraits of Washington*, no. 210; Baker, *Engraved Portraits of Washington*, no. 130; Wick, *American Icon*, no. 63). The engraving is noted also by David McNeely Stauffer, *American Engravers Upon Copper and Steel* (New York: The Grolier Club, 1907), no. 1466. *The Boston Magazine* 1 (1784), frontispiece (Hart, *Engraved Portraits of Washington*, no. 57; Stauffer, *American Engravers*, no. 2353; Wick, *American Icon*, no. 19). Wick, *American Icon*, 93; quoted by Wick, *American Icon*, 93.

55. *The Monthly Military Repository* (1796) (Hart, *Engraved Portraits of Washington*, no. 248; Baker, *Engraved Portraits of Washington*, no. 173; Stauffer, *American Engravers*, no. 3257; Wick, *American Icon*, no. 43); *The American Universal Magazine* 1 (1797) (Hart, *Engraved Portraits of Washington*, no. 171; Baker, *Engraved Portraits of Washington,* no. 89; Wick, *American Icon*, no. 49). The editors' comment is quoted by Wick, *American Icon*, 118; *The South Carolina Weekly Museum* 1 (1797), title page (Wick, *American Icon*, no. 50). *Connecticut Magazine* 1 (1801), frontispiece, stipple by Amos Doolittle (Hart, *Engraved Portraits of Washington*, no. 507; Baker, *Engraved Portraits of Washington,* no. 204; Stauffer, *American Engravers*, no. 520); *The Literary Casket and Pocket Magazine* (1822), frontispiece, stipple by Gimbrede (Hart, *Engraved Portraits of Washington*, no. 510b; Stauffer, *American Engravers*, no. 1099).

56. Hart, *Engraved Portraits of Washington*, no. 776; Stauffer, *American Engravers*, no. 1689; Wick, *American Icon*, no. 65.

57. *The Philadelphia Magazine and Review, or, Monthly Repository and Amusement* 1 (1799), v.

58. Patricia A. Anderson, *Promoted to Glory: The Apotheosis of George Washington* (Northampton, MA: Smith College Museum of Art, 1980), 11.

59. George Richardson, *Iconology; or, A Collection of Emblematical Figures* (London: G. Scott, 1779), book 2, 31; ibid., book 1, 39; ibid., book 3, 53.

60. Wick, *American Icon*, 135.

61. *Philadelphia Repertory* 1 (1810), frontispiece (Hart, *Engraved Portraits of Washington*, no. 509; Stauffer, *American Engravers*, no. 1007).

Davida Tenenbaum Deutsch examines Folwell's career in "Samuel Folwell of Philadelphia: An Artist for the Needleworker," *Antiques* 119 (1981), 420–23. Richardson, *Iconology*, book 3, 73; ibid., 16.

62. Mott, *History of American Magazines*, 320–30; *The New York Mirror: A Weekly Journal* 9 (1831), title page (Stauffer, *American Engravers*, no. 663).

63. *The Port Folio* 5 (1811), 281–83. The engraving was executed by George Murray, according to Mott, *History of American Magazines*, 209. I have not been able to substantiate the claim in Hart, Baker or Stauffer.

64. *The Boston Magazine* 1 (1784), facing 221; after Copley (Cresswell, *American Revolution in Drawings and Prints*, no. 204).

65. *The Columbian Magazine: or, Monthly Miscellany* 1 (1786), frontispiece (Stauffer, *American Engravers*, no. 3274; Cresswell, *American Revolution in Drawings and Prints*, no. 99).

66. *The Columbian Magazine* 1 (1786), 1.

67. *The Boston Magazine* 1 (1784), facing 221; after Copley (Cresswell, *American Revolution in Drawings and Prints*, no. 204); *The Columbian Magazine: or, Monthly Miscellany* 1 (1786), frontispiece (Stauffer, *American Engravers*, no. 3274; Cresswell, *American Revolution in Drawings and Prints*, no. 99); *The Columbian Magazine* 1 (1786), 1; *National Magazine* 1 (1799), 84–87, 140–45.

68. Allen, *An American Biographical and Historical Dictionary*, 490–91. See chapter 3 for a discussion of the use of the tale in schoolbooks. *Columbian Magazine: or, Monthly Miscellany* 2 (1788), 591–92; *Philadelphia Repertory* 1(1810), 177–78.

69. *Polyanthos* 1 (1806), 120–21.

70. *Ohio Miscellaneous Museum* 1 (1822), 190–91. The original appears in Mason Locke Weems, *The Life of Gen. Francis Marion,* 4th ed. (Philadelphia: M. Carey, 1816), 156–60. *Southern Review* 1 (1828), 70–105.

71. *New York Magazine, or Literary Repository* 2 (1797), 113–15. Benjamin Tanner engraved the portrait (Stauffer, *American Engravers*, no. 3108). This biographical sketch, without the portrait, appeared also in the *Literary Museum* (1797), 98–99. *Polyanthos* 2 (1806), 217–22 (Stauffer, *American Engravers*, no. 1275); *The Port Folio* 1 (1809), 402–8.

72. *The Port Folio* 2 (1809), facing 285 (Stauffer, *American Engravers*, no. 714); *The Port Folio* 1 (1809), facing 402 (Stauffer, *American Engravers*, no. 909); *The Port Folio* 2 (1809), frontispiece (Stauffer, *American Engravers*, no. 767).

73. *The Port Folio* 8 (1812), facing 101 (Stauffer, *American Engravers*, no. 832); *The Port Folio* 6 (1811), facing 383 (Stauffer, *American Engravers*,

no. 797). Both were taken from paintings by Charles Willson Peale. The engraving of Morgan copies Peale's 1794 of the general (Charles Coleman Sellers, *Portraits and Miniatures by Charles Willson Peale*. Transactions of the American Philosophical Society, Vol 42, Part 1 [1952; reprint, Philadelphia: American Philosophical Society, 1968], no. 568); the engraving of Knox repeats a Peale miniature of 1778 (Sellers, *Portraits and Miniatures*, no. 440).

74. *The Port Folio* 6 (1811), 108. Less noteworthy biographical sketches of Knox appeared in two short-lived periodicals, *Omnium Gatherum* 1 (1810) and *The New Jersey Monthly Magazine* 1 (1825).

75. *The Port Folio* 3 (1810), 81–86. Leney engraved a portrait of Schuyler to accompany this biography (Stauffer, *American Engravers*, no. 1848).

76. Quoted by Mott, *History of American Magazines*, 222.

77. For example, the *Port Folio*, one of the most successful magazines of the period, had a circulation of 2000. *The Monthly Anthology*, on the other hand, had a circulation of only 440 in 1805. See Mott, *History of American Magazines*, 199–200. Michael T. Gilmore, "The Literature of the Revolutionary and Early National Periods," in *The Cambridge History of American Literature*, ed. Sacvan Bercovitch (Cambridge: Cambridge Univ. Press, 1994), 1:558–61.

78. Morse, *The American Geography*; Noah Webster, *Little Reader's Assistant* (Hartford: Elisha Babcock, 1790), 32–37. I base these remarks on a survey of 237 early American schoolbooks in the collections of Harvard University, the American Antiquarian Society, and the Boston Public Library. These collections do not include some of the texts listed in the four bibliographies of schoolbooks that have been published since the nineteenth century. On the other hand, the collections do contain schoolbooks that are not listed in any of these four bibliographies. The most comprehensive of the bibliographies is: "American Schoolbooks," *American Journal of Education*, "A–C," 13 (1863), 209–22; "D–G," 13 (1863), 626–40; "H–O," 14 (1864), 753–77; "O–Z," 15 (1865), 539–75. The other three bibliographies of early American schoolbooks can be found in Oscar Adolph Tinglestad, "The Religious Element in American School Readers up to 1830" (Ph.D. diss. Univ. of Chicago, 1925); R. L. Delmolen, *A Bibliography of United States History Textbooks, 1820–1825, Including an Examination of Their Treatment by John A. Nietz* (Ann Arbor: Ann Arbor Publishers, 1962); and Ruth Elson, *Guardians of Tradition: American Schoolbooks of the Nineteenth Century* (Lincoln: Univ. of Nebraska Press, 1964).

79. William J. Gilmore explores the impact of the increase in rural educational institutions in *Reading Becomes a Necessity of Life: Material and Cultural Life in Rural New England, 1780–1835* (Knoxville: Univ. of

Tennessee Press, 1989), 356–58. Jack Larkin, "The Merriams of Brookfield: Printing in the Economy and Culture of Rural Massachusetts in the Early Nineteenth Century," *Proceedings of the American Antiquarian Society* 96 (1986), 67. The importance of schoolbooks in the printer's inventory is noted also by Philip F. Gura, "Early Nineteenth-Century Printing in Rural Massachusetts: John Howe of Greenwich and Enfield, c. 1803–1845," in *The Crossroads of American History and Literature* (University Park, PA: Pennsylvania State Univ. Press, 1996), 134. Charles Carpenter, *History of American Schoolbooks* (Philadelphia: Univ. of Pennsylvania Press, 1963), 62.

80. Gilmore discusses the moral aspects of reading lessons in *Reading Becomes a Necessity of Life*, 37–40. Moral tales were also prominent in children's literature of the period. See Gail S. Murray, "Rational Thought and Republican Virtues: Children's Literature, 1789–1820," *Journal of the Early Republic* 8 (1988), 159–77.

81. Weems ensured, as best he could, that illustrations accompanied editions of all his pamphlets. As well as in his lives of Washington, Marion, Penn, and Franklin, frontispieces were included in *Hymen's Recruiting-Serjeant, God's Revenge Against Murder, God's Revenge Against Gambling*, and *The Drunkard's Looking Glass*.

82. William Scott, *Lessons in Elocution: or, a Selection of Pieces, in Prose and Verse, for the Improvement of Youth in Reading and Speaking*, 15th American Edition (Hartford, 1806); [Caleb Bingham], *American Preceptor, Being a New Selection of Lessons for Reading and Speaking*, Second Walpole Edition (Walpole, NH: Thomas & Thomas, 1802). See David Hall, "Introduction: The Uses of Literacy in New England, 1600–1850," *Printing and Society in Early America*, ed. William L. Joyce, David D. Hall, Richard D. Brown, and John B. Hench (Worcester: American Antiquarian Society, 1983), 21–22. John A. Nietz offers the unlikely explanation that readers "emphasized the mastery of effective oral reading" because the "democratic political development of our country required public speaking on the part of the candidates and their friends. *Old Textbooks* ([Pittsburg:] Univ. of Pittsburg Press, 1961), 61. William J. Gilmore discusses methods of teaching reading in *Reading Becomes a Necessity of Life: Material and Cultural Life in Rural New England, 1780–1835* (Knoxville: Univ. of Tennessee Press, 1989), 34–42. Samuel Read Hall, *Lectures to School-Masters, on Teaching*, 4th ed. (Boston: Hendee & Co., 1833), 87–89.

83. Scott, *Lessons in Elocution*, 9, 5. Arthur O. Lovejoy discusses neoclassical conceptions of nature and art in "'Nature' as Aesthetic Norm," *Essays in the History of Ideas* (Baltimore: The Johns Hopkins Press, 1948), 69–

77. See also Walter Jackson Bate, *From Classic to Romantic: Premises of Taste in Eighteenth-Century England* (Cambridge, MA: Harvard Univ. Press, 1946), chapter 29. Scott, *Lessons in Elocution*, 15, 4; James Burgh, *The Art of Speaking,* 2nd ed. (London: n.p., 1763); John Walker, *Academic Speaker,* 4th London Edition (London: n.p., 1801). [Bingham], *American Preceptor,* 57. The source of these instructions was Hugh Blair's well-known *Lectures on Rhetoric and Belles Lettres.*

84. Scott, *Lessons in Elocution*, 204–5.

85. [Bingham], *American Preceptor,* 171–73.

86. [Bingham], *American Preceptor,* 11; ibid., 30–31;Scott, *Lessons in Elocution*, 90.

87. Scott, *Lessons in Elocution*, 92; [Bingham], *American Preceptor*, 77–79.

88. Scott, *Lessons in Elocution*, 94; [Bingham], *American Preceptor*, 104.

89. Michael V. Belok makes an unconvincing attempt to relate the schoolbook emphasis on virtue with the courtesy book tradition. He believes readers and primers were "a special type of courtesy book" (*Forming the American Minds: Early School Books and their Compilers 1783–1837* [Moti Katra, India: Satish Book Enterprise, 1973], 56). John Pierpont's texts were a notable exception to the conventional practice of beginning with instructions on rhetorical technique. Pierpont wrote, "The truth probably is that reading like conversation is learned from example rather than by rule" (*American First Class Book; or, Exercises in Reading and Recitation* (Boston: W. B. Fowle, 1823), preface. Rudolph R. Reeder briefly discusses the significance of Pierpont in *The Historical Development of School Readers and of Method in Teaching Reading,* Columbia Univ. Contributions to Philosophy, Psychology and Education, no. 2 (New York: Columbia Univ., 1900).

90. Weems to Carey, February 23, 1809, 2:393.

91. Weems to Thomas Jefferson, February 1, 1809, 2:389; Weems, *The Life of George Washington,* 183–84.

92. Weems, *History of General George Washington,* 22–28; ibid., 38; ibid., 22–28.

93. Weems, *History of General George Washington,* 28–36; Robert Beverley, *The History and Present State of Virginia* (1705; reprint, ed. Louis B. Wright, Chapel Hill: Univ. of North Carolina Press, 1947), book 4, chapter 19; J. Hector St. John de Crevecoeur, *Letters from an American Farmer* (1782; reprint, New York: E.P. Dutton, 1957), 154; quoted by Arthur H. Shaffer, introduction to *History of Virginia,* by Edmund Randolph, ed. Arthur H. Shaffer (Charlottesville: Univ. Press of Virginia, 1970), 72. Environmental

theories are discussed also by Cohen, *The Revolutionary Histories*, 121–24, and Ralph Norman Miller, "The Historians Discover America: A Study of American Historical Writing in the Eighteenth Century" (Ph.D. diss., Northwestern Univ., 1946).

94. Weems, *The Life of George Washington*, 208–9.

95. Weems, *The Life of George Washington*, 213–14; ibid., 205–6.

96. Weems played upon the conventional juxtaposition of sloth with industry when, complaining of a late delivery of books, he informed Carey: "I begin to grow feverish. That vile aquatic Sloth, nicknamed The Industry is not yet arrived! But for her crew and cargo I would not weep were she at moorings in Davy Jones's locker, or tho the Ferryman of hell had her to put Austrians across the styx." Weems to Carey, September 20, 1796, 2:37; Weems, *Life of George Washington*, 212. The contrast between the benefits of industry and the dire consequences of idleness was a commonplace in children's literature of the period. Maria Edgeworth's "Lazy Lawrence; or Industry and Idleness Contrasted" was the most well known and often imitated story based on characters who represent industry and idleness. The story found its way into Samuel Putnam's *The Introduction to the Analytical Reader . . .* (Salem: Whipple and Lawrence, 1828), and variations on it occurred in numerous readers. See, for instance, Joab G. Cooper, *The North American Spelling-Book; or the Youth's Instructer* (Philadelphia: Towar, J. & D. M. Hogan, and Pittsburg: Hogan & Co., 1830) and [Sarah Preston Hale], *Boston Reading Lessons* (Boston: Richardson, Lord & Holbrook, 1830). In her study of American children's literature, Kiefer examines the use of the story in Sunday school tracts such as *Take Your Choice; or the Difference between Virtue and Vice, Shown in Opposite Characters* (Philadelphia, 1804). For an excellent discussion of the industry and idleness theme in eighteenth-century English literature and art, with special attention to Hogarth, see Ronald Paulson, *Emblem and Expression: Meaning in English Art of the Eighteenth Century* (Cambridge, MA: Harvard Univ. Press, 1975), chapter 5.

97. Scott, *Lessons in Elocution*, 79; Elihu F. Marshall, *A Spelling Book of the English Language* (Wells River, VT: Ira White, 1830), 92–93. This selection without its illustration occurs in Rensselaer Bently, *The American Instructer*, 4th ed. (Bennington, VT: Darius Clark, 1829), and Asa Rhoads, *New Instructor, being the Second Part of the American Spelling Book* (Stanford, CT: Daniel Lawrence, 1803). An interesting variant may be found in William Collier, *The Evangelical Instructor: Designed for the Use of Schools and Families* (Boston: Richardson & Lord, 1821), in which "the special hand of Providence" has given the sloth uses which include being a mirror to "The man

who lives only to eat and drink; to indulge his appetite, to feast his flesh, to dose away his life in sleepy inactivity, and to consume himself (his nobler self, his soul) and his substance, in wretched indolence, and bodily indulgencies" (157). Herman Daggett's *The American Reader: Consisting of Familiar, Instructive, and Entertaining Stories* (Sag Harbor, NY: Alden Spooner, 1806) includes an allegorical reading of the sloth.

98. *Portico* 2 (1816), 292. In his study of New England reading instruction, *Reading Becomes a Necessity of Life*, William J. Gilmore does not mention Weems' work, nor the use of other book-length biographies.

99. [James Jones Wilmer], *The American Nepos: A Collection of the Lives of the Most Remarkable and the Most Eminent Men, Who Have Contributed to the Recovery, the Settlement, and the Independence of America. Calculated for the Use of Schools* (Baltimore: G. Douglas, 1805), frontispiece, stipple by Scoles. Wick reproduces frontispieces of three editions of Webster: *An American Selection of Lessons in Reading and Speaking*, 3rd ed. (Philadelphia: Young and M'Culloch, 1787); *The American Spelling-Book*, 7th ed. (Philadelphia: Young and M'Culloch, 1787); and *The American Spelling Book*, 14th ed. (New York: Campbell, 1792) (Wick, *American Icon*, no. 22 and no. 32). Wick also cites three other possible occurrences of frontispieces in Webster textbooks that are now unlocated. Emily Ellsworth Ford Skeel writes that Webster initially objected to using a portrait of Washington because he believed it disrespectful, but later changed his mind and sought to control the printers' use of the frontispiece (*The Bibliography of the Writings of Noah Webster*, ed. Edwin H. Carpenter, Jr. (New York: New York Public Library and Arno Press, 1958), 11). Wick also includes a crude frontispiece from a 1797 edition of *The New-England Primer* (Wick, *American Icon*, no. 51). Weems to Carey, March 25, 1809, 2:397. For examples of the prevalence of frontispieces, see Wick, *American Icon*.

100. Weems to Carey, June 24, 1799, 1:between 2 and 3; Weems, *The Life and Memorable Actions of George Washington . . .* ([Baltimore:] Keatinge, [1800]), frontispiece (Wick, *American Icon*, no. 91).

101. Weems to Carey, February 2, 1800, 2:127; A *History*, 2nd ed. (Philadelphia: John Bioren, [1800], frontispiece (Hart, *Engraved Portraits of Washington*, no. 524; Baker, *Engraved Portraits of Washington*, no. 338; Stauffer, *American Engravers*, no. 3103; Wick, *American Icon*, no. 92).

102. Weems to Carey, July 10, 1800, 2:131; ibid., July 12, 1800, 2:132; ibid., August 25, 1800, 2:141–42. The practice of using a portrait of someone other than Washington is addressed in "Academy of Fine Arts: Remarks on Portraits of General Washington, 1824," 26–27. Weems, *History* of . . .

W*ashington,* 3rd ed. (Philadelphia: Bioren, [1800], frontispiece (Hart, *Engraved Portraits of Washington,* no. 523; Baker, *Engraved Portraits of Washington,* no. 340; Stauffer, *American Engravers,* no. 3106; Wick, *American Icon,* no. 93).

103. Weems to Carey, August 12, 1809, 2:418; Weems, *The Life of George Washington.* . . , 8th ed. (Philadelphia, 1809). The plates are: 'Death of General Montgomery,' frontispiece; 'Defeat of General Braddock,' 40; 'Battle of Lexington,' 70; 'Battle of Bunker's Hill & Death of Gen. Warren,' 77; 'Capture of Major Andre,' 105; and 'Surrender of Lord Cornwallis,' 114. See also Randolph G. Adams, "The Historical Illustrations in Weems's Washington," *The Colophon,* part 8 (1931), n. p.

104. Rosemary Freeman, *English Emblem Books* (London: Chatto & Windus, 1948), chapter 1.

105. Geffery Whitney, *A Choice of Emblemes,* ed. Henry Greene (1586; reprint, London: Lovell Reeves and Co., 1866), 215.

106. Freeman, *English Emblem Books,* 15, 204–28; Paulson, *Emblem and Expression.*

107. Maria E. Skidmore, "The American Emblem Book and its Symbolism" (Ph.D. diss., Ohio State Univ., 1947); John Owen Rees, Jr., "Hawthorne and the Emblem" (Ph.D. diss., State Univ. of Iowa, 1965).

108. *The New England Primer, improved* . . . (New York, 1794), and *The New England Primer, improved* . . . (Brattleborough, 1825), quoted in Paul Leicester Ford, ed. *The New England Primer. A History of its Origin and Development* (New York: Dodd, Mead and Company, 1897), 25. Wick does not cite the 1794 edition.

109. *The New England Primer: Much Improved* (Germantown, 1796); reprinted by Wick, *American Icon,* 116.

110. This text and subsequent schoolbook histories developed as specialized readers. Although they dispensed with formal instruction on rhetorical technique, schoolbook histories continued the practice of using lessons brief enough to be declaimed in class. Furthermore, authors of these texts were as concerned with the effects of rhetoric on children as the authors of readers.

111. *The History of America Abridged for the Use of Children* (Philadelphia: Curtis, 1795); Wick, *American Icon,* no. 41; Sinclair Hamilton, *Early American Book Illustrators and Wood Engravers 1670–1870* (Princeton: Princeton Univ. Press, 1958), no. 160.

112. [Samuel Griswold Goodrich], *The First Book of History, for Children and Youth* (Boston: Richardson, Lord & Holbrook, 1831), 112–13. A similar relief cut modeled after Trumbull's *Battle of Bunker's Hill* occurs in Samuel

Goodrich's *The Tales* of *Peter Parley, About America* (Boston: S. G. Goodrich, 1827), 115.

113. Washington's exemplary industriousness, benevolence, piety, humility, honesty, equanimity, courage and patriotism were extolled in: Jedidiah Morse, *The American Geography*; Nathaniel Heaton, Jr., *The Columbian Preceptor* (Wrentham [MA]: Nathaniel Heaton, 1801), 153–56; [Wilmer], 382–84; Asa Lyman, *The American Reader,* 2nd ed. (Portland, ME: A. Lyman & Co., 1811), 60–66; Joseph Richardson, *Young Ladies' Selection of Elegant Extracts from the Writings of Illustrious Females* (Boston: John Eliot, 1811), 193–94; Increase Cooke, *Introduction to the American Orator, or, a New Selection of Lessons in Reading and Speaking* (New Haven: Increase Cooke and Co., 1812), 142–48; Joseph Hutton, *The New American Reader* (Philadelphia: David Hogan, 1813), 105; Rodolphus Dickinson, *The Columbian Reader* (Boston: R. P. & C. Williams, and Hallowell [ME]: Ezekiel Goodale, 1815), 109; J. P. Slack, *The American Orator* (Trenton, NJ: D. Fenton, 1815), 250–51; M. R. Bartlett, *The Practical Reader in Five Books* (New York: Myers and Smith, 1823), 272–73; [George Merriam ?], *The American Reader* (Boston: Pierce & Williams, and Brookfield [MA]: E. and G. Merriam, 1828), 223–25; Jesse Olney, *The National Preceptor, or, Selections in Poetry and Prose . . .* (Hartford: Goodwin & Co, 1830), 23–27; M. R. Bartlett, *The Common School Manual: A Regular and Connected Course of Elementary Studies . . . Part III* (Utica: William Williams, 1828) and *The National School Manual,* 2nd ed. (Philadelphia: Carey & Lea, 1832), 106. Rufus Adams, *The Young Gentleman and Lady's Explanatory Monitor* (Danville, VT: n.p., 1808), 129; Albert Picket, *The Juvenile Mentor* (Wheeling, WV: A. & E. Picket, 1825), 97–99; John Pierpont, *Introduction to the National Reader* (Boston: Richardson and Lord, 1828), 76–79; and Lydia Maria Child, *Biographical Sketches of Great and Good Men,* 2nd ed. (Boston: Putnam & Hunt, 1829), 29–30.

114. [Wilmer], 254–55; [Bingham], *The American Preceptor,* 96–97.

115. Webster, *Little Reader's Assistant,* 34; *Juvenile Miscellany* (Boston: John Putnam, 1827), facing 290.

116. Benjamin Rush, *A Plan for the Establishment of Public Schools and the Diffusion of Knowledge in Pennsylvania to Which Are Added, Thoughts upon the Mode of Education, Proper in a Republic. Addressed to the Legislature and Citizens of the State* (Philadelphia, 1786), in *Essays on Education in the Early Republic,* ed. Frederick Rudolph (Cambridge, MA: Harvard Univ. Press, 1965), 14.

117. Elson, 187; Roscoe R. Robinson, *Two Centuries of Change in the Content of School Readers,* Contributions to Education of George Peabody College for Teachers, no. 59 (Nashville: George Peabody College, 1930), 18, 27.

118. *Practical Reading Lessons on the Three Great Virtues* (Baltimore: Lucas & 1830), 112–13.

119. Robert E. Cray. Jr. argues that patrician attitudes toward heroes and virtue helped create and perpetuate admiration for Andre in the United States. Cray examines the restoration of status to Andre's captors and its effect on perceptions of Revolutionary soldiers. "Major Andre and the Three Captors: Class Dynamics and Revolutionary Memory Wars in the Early Republic, 1780–1831," *Journal of the Early Republic* 17 (1997), 371–97.

120. Olney, *The National Preceptor,* 47–48; A. T. Lowe, *Second Class Book; Principally Consisting of Historical, Geographical, and Biographical Lessons* (Brookfield, MA: E. and G. Merriam, 1825), 58–61; J. L. Blake, *The Juvenile Companion, Being an Introduction to the Historical Reader* (Boston: Bowles and Dearborne, 1827), 199–203. The details of Andre's execution were also recounted in James M'Allaster, *The Schools Instructor* (Middlebury [VT]: 1810), 22–36. Brief mention of Andre's capture and execution occur in Noah Webster, *Elements of Useful Knowledge. Vol I. Containing a Historical and Geographical Account of the United States: For the Use of Schools,* 4th ed. (Hartford: Hudson & Goodwin, 1813), 48; [Josiah Hook], *The Practical Expositor, and Sententious Reader* (Gardner [MA]: P. Sheldon, 1829), 194; and a number of American histories written especially for schoolchildren. These histories include: Salma Hale, *History of the United States . . . to the Close of the War with Great Britain in 1815* (New York: N. White, 1815), 190; [Charles Prentiss], *History of the United States of America . . . For the Use of Schools and Private Families,* 2nd ed. (Keene, NH: J. Prentiss, 1820), 159–60; William Grimshaw, *History of the United States,* 3rd ed. (Philadelphia, n.p., 1822), 168–69; Charles A. Goodrich, *A History of the United States of America* (Hartford: Huntington and Hopkins, 1823), 215–17; and Samuel Williams, *A History of the American Revolution: Intended as a Reading-Book for Schools* (New Haven: W. Storer, Jr., 1824), 149–52.

121. Joseph Richardson, *The American Reader: A Selection of Lessons for Reading and Speaking. Wholly from American Authors* (Boston: Lincoln & Edmands, 1810), 92; *Stories about Arnold and Champe* (New Haven: n.p., 1831), 50–51.

122. The literature on the growth of American nationalism is extensive. Among the general surveys that I have found most helpful are: Stephen Watts,

The Republic Reborn: War and the Making of Liberal America, 1790–1820 (Baltimore: The Johns Hopkins Univ. Press, 1987); David Waldstreicher, *In the Midst of Perpetual Fetes: The Making of American Nationalism, 1776–1820* (Chapel Hill: Univ. of North Carolina Press, 1997); George Dangerfield, *The Awakening of American Nationalism 1815–1828* (New York: Harper & Row, 1965); Richard W. Van Alstyne, *Genesis of American Nationalism* (Waltham, MA: Blaisdell Publishing Company, 1970); and Paul C. Nagel, *This Sacred Trust: American Nationality, 1798–1898* (New York: Oxford Univ. Press, 1971). On cultural nationalism, see Benjamin T. Spencer, *The Quest for Nationality*; Russel Blaine Nye, *The Cultural Life of the New Nation 1776–1830* (New York: Harper & Row, 1960); and Neil Harris, *The Artist in America.*

123. Hannah Adams, *An Abridgement of the History of New England, for the Use of Young Persons* (Boston: n.p., 1805), 158–60. This is the earliest anecdote of Hale's execution that I have found. Adams claims (160, note) to have been told the story's details by Gen. Hull of Newton, Massachusetts. The story of Hale's death occurs also in Pierpont, *Introduction to the National Reader,* 133–35, and Webster, *Elements of Useful Knowledge,* 33–34. Hale's stature as a hero of the Revolution may have been slow to grow. Four years later William Allen did not include Hale in his *American Biographical and Historical Dictionary.*

124. Joshua Leavitt, *Easy Lessons in Reading* (Keene, NH: John Prentiss, 1823), 143; [Samuel Putnam], *Lessons in Simultaneous Reading, Spelling, and Defining* (Portsmith: T. H. Miller, 1826), 6–9; Thomas J. Lee, *Primary Class Book* (Hallowell [ME]: Glazier, Masters & Co., [c. 1827]), 43–44; Israel Alger, *The Orthoepical Guide to the English Tongue* (Boston: Richardson and Lord, 1829), 107–8; The *National Spelling Book, and Scholars Guide* (Concord, NH: Charles Hoag, 1829), 89–91; Lyman Cobb, *Cobb's Juvenile Reader, No. 2* (Oxford, NY: Chapman & Flager, 1832), 111–12; Joseph Richardson, *The American Reader,* 93–97; Samuel Temple, *The Child's Assistant in the Art of Reading,* 5th ed. (Boston: Lincoln & Edmands, 1816), 84–85; A. T. Lowe, *The Columbian Class Book, Consisting of Geographical, Historical and Biographical Extracts* (Worcester: Dorr & Howland, 1824), 13; Noah Worcester, *Friend of Youth; or New Selection of Lessons, in Prose and Verse, for Schools and Families,* 2nd ed. (Boston: Cummings, Hilliard, and Co., 1823), 218–19; [Samuel Putnam], *Lessons,* 76; *The Analytical Reader,* 2nd ed. (Dover, NH: Samuel C. Stevens, 1827), 78–80.

125. William Biglow, *The Youth's Library. A Selection of Lessons in Reading. Vol. I* (Salem: Cushing and Appleton, 1803), 55–58. A variation of

this story appears also in [John Kingston], *The Reader's Cabinet* (Baltimore: John Kingston, 1809), 88–89.

126. Samuel Goodrich, *The First Book of History*, 110. The comparison also occurs in the Boston magazine *Polyanthos* 1 (1806), 228; Bartlett, *Common School Manual*, 480; ibid., 497.

127. Charles A. Goodrich, *History of the United States of America* (New York: A. K. White, 1829), 205; Bartlett, *Common School Manual*, 482; Grimshaw, *History of the United States*, 180; Bartlett, ibid., 505.

128. Salma Hale, *History of the United States*, 142.

129. Mrs. [Caroline Matilda] Thayer, *First Lessons in the History of the United States, Compiled for the Use of the Junior Classes in Joseph Hoxie's Academy* (New York: D. Fanshaw, 1823), 67–68; Richardson, *The American Reader*, 72; Joseph Chandler, *The Young Gentleman and Lady's Museum* (Hallowell, ME: N. Cheever, 1811), 148; Salma Hale, *History of the United States*, 154–55. Montgomery's death is recounted also in [B. R. Evans], *The Republican Compiler* (Pittsburg, n.p., 1818), 85.

130. See Watt, *Republic Reborn*, 163–64; Peter S. Onuf, "State Politics and Republican Virtue: Religion, Education, and Morality in Early American Federalism," in *Toward a Usable Past: Liberty Under State Constitutions*, ed. Paul Finkelman and Stephen E. Gottlieb (Athens: Univ. of Georgia Press, 1991), 101–8; Waldstreicher, *In the Midst of Perpetual Fetes*, 73. Noah Webster, *On the Education of Youth in America* (1787–88; 1790), in *Essays on Education in the Early Republic*, 65; Bolingbroke, "Letters on the Study and Use of History," 326.

131. Heaton, *The Columbian Preceptor*, 153–54; *American Museum* 11 (1792), 44–45; *The Juvenile Magazine* 1 (1802), 15; Wilson, *Biography of Principle Military and Naval Heroes*, 1:6; Ramsay, *Life of George Washington*, dedication page; *The Polyanthos* 3 (1814), 216.

132. On the emergence of enterprise as a dominant force in American life, see Gordon S. Wood, *The Radicalism of the American Revolution* (New York: Alfred A. Knopf, 1992), especially 325–47; Watts, *Republic Reborn*; Waldstreicher, *In the Midst of Perpetual Fetes*; Joyce Appleby, *Capitalism and a New Social Order: The Republican Vision of the 1790s* (New York and London: New York Univ. Press, 1984); and Robert A. Ferguson, "The American Enlightenment, 1750–1820," in *The Cambridge History of American Literature*, ed. Sacvan Bercovitch (Cambridge: Cambridge Univ. Press, 1994), 1:534–37. The anachronistic nature of classical republican virtues during the period is discussed in Linda Kerber, *Federalists in Dissent: Imagery and Ideology in Jeffersonian America* (Ithaca: Cornell Univ. Press, 1970); Henry F.

May, *The Enlightenment in America* (New York: Oxford Univ. Press, 1976); Rowland Berthoff, "Independence and Attachment, Virtue and Interest: From Republican Citizen to Free Enterpriser," *Uprooted Americans: Essays in Honor of Oscar Handlin*, ed. Richard L. Bushman et al. (Boston: Little, Brown, 1979), 991–24. Ramsay quoted in Ferguson, "The American Enlightenment, 1750–1820," 535; Mercy Otis Warren, *History of the Rise, Progress, and Termination of the American Revolution. Interspersed with Biographical, Political and Moral Observations* . . . (Boston: Manning and Loring, 1805), 4; quoted in Watts, *Republic Reborn*, 73, 220.

133. *Weekly Register* 1 (1811), 70; Thomas Jones Rogers, *New American Biographical Dictionary; or, Remembrancer of the Departed Heroes, Sages and Statesmen of America. Confined Exclusively to Those Who Signalized Themselves in Either Capacity, in the Revolutionary War*, 3rd ed. (Easton, PA: T. J. Rogers, 1824), iii–iv; *The Port Folio* 3 (1810), 86; quoted in Waldstreicher, *In the Midst of Perpetual Fetes*, 58.

134. Humphreys, *Life of the Honorable Major-General Israel Putnam*, 1013; Caldwell, *Life and Campaigns of the Hon. Nathaniel Greene*, x, xii, xv. Waldstreicher notes that "Many of the partisan battles of the decade [1790s] fused or confused the issue of participation in public life with questions of individual and national integrity. Thus it was not that individual manhood was on the line. The issue is more complicated because the nation was theorized and discussed in terms of the individual: that is, the very language used to discuss the national polity involved personifying tropes like 'national character. . . . both nation and state had a reputation, a character, to establish." *In the Midst of Perpetual Fetes*, 125. *Southern Review* 1 (1828), 105.

135. *The Massachusetts Magazine* 2 (1790), 453–54; "On the Use of Books for Children," *American Journal of Education* 1 (1831), 103–5; "On Books for Children," *American Journal of Education* 1(1828), 100–1.

136. Elizabeth Barnes, exploring concepts of sympathy in the early American novel, concentrates on Adam Smith's *The Theory of Moral Sentiments* and the problem of sympathetic identification. Barnes writes that Smith provides "a model of sympathetic relations as both fundamentally self-interested and imaginative in nature." More broadly, Barnes argues that sympathetic identification "emerges in the eighteenth century as the definitive way of reading literature and human relations." My conclusions about the influence of Scottish Enlightenment theories of sympathy more narrowly focus on ideas concerning the impact on the reader of narratives of virtuous action. See Elizabeth Barnes, *States of Sympathy: Seduction and Democracy in the American Novel* (New York: Columbia Univ. Press, 1997), chapter 1. Gordon

Wood demonstrates the growing importance, and cultural implications, of being able to share feelings with others in *Radicalism of the American Revolution*, 218–25

137. Joseph Addison, *Spectator Essay No. 420*, in *Selections from The Tatler and The Spectator of Steele and Addison*, ed. Angus Ross (New York: Penguin Books, n.d.), 398.

138. Kenneth Silverman discusses its popularity in A *Cultural History of the Revolution: Painting, Music, Literature and the Theatre in the Colonies and the United States from the Treaty of Paris to the Inauguration of George Washington, 1763–1789* (New York: Thomas Y. Crowell, 1976), 131, 365, 505. Joseph Addison, *Cato, A Tragedy*, in *A Select Collection of English Plays* (Edinburgh, 1755), 4.

139. Francis Hutcheson, whose work is tangential to my argument, developed Addison's ideas and was an important precursor to Hume. "The word moral goodness," Hutcheson wrote, "denotes our idea of some quality apprehended in actions, which procures approbation. . . . " Hutcheson argued that there were three ethical senses: the public, the moral, and the sense of honor. Hume replaced Hutcheson's triad with sympathy as the primary moral sense. See Francis Hutchenson, *An Inquiry Concerning Beauty, Order, Harmony, Design*, ed. Peter Kivy (The Hague: Martinus Nijhoff, 1973) and Walter John Hipple, Jr., *The Beautiful, the Sublime, & the Picturesque in Eighteenth-Century British Aesthetic Theory* (Carbondale: The Southern Illinois Univ. Press, 1957). Although Hipple concentrates on the aesthetic categories listed in his title, his book is the most comprehensive survey I have found of the writers under discussion. David Hume, *Treatise of Human Nature*, ed. L. A. Selby-Bigge (Oxford: Clarendon Press, 1896), 316; ibid., 1; ibid., 317.

140. Ibid., 319.

141. Hipple, *The Beautiful, the Sublime, & the Picturesque*, 67.

142. Alexander Gerard, *An Essay on Taste*, (1759; reprint, ed. Walter J. Hipple, Jr., Gainesville, FL: Scholar's Facsimiles & Reprints, 1963), 185; ibid., 186.

143. Henry Home, Lord Kames, *The Elements of Criticism*, 6th ed. (Edinburgh, 1785), 1:93, 63, 65.

144. John Ogilvie, *Philosophical and Critical Observations on the Nature, Character and Various Species of Composition* (London, 1774), 1:112–13; Joseph Priestley, *A Course of Lectures on Oratory and Criticism*, (1777; reprint, ed. Vincent M. Bevilacqua and Richard Murphy, Carbondale: Southern Illinois Univ. Press, 1965), 27–28; Hugh Blair, *Lectures on Rhetoric and Belles*

Lettres (1783; reprint, ed. Harold F. Harding, Carbondale: Southern Illinois Univ. Press, 1965), 2:281–82, 274.

145. On rhetoric in college see William Chavat, *The Origins of American Critical Thought 1810–1835* (Philadelphia: Univ. of Pennsylvania Press, 1936), 31–33; Warren Guthrie, "The Development of Rhetorical Theory in America, 1635–1850," *Speech Monographs* 15 (1948), 61–71; Vincent Freimarck, "Rhetoric at Yale in 1807," *Proceedings of the American Philosophical Society* 110 (1966), 235–55; David S. Shields, "British-American Belles Lettres," in *The Cambridge History of American Literature*, ed. Sacvan Bercovitch (Cambridge: Cambridge Univ. Press, 1994), 1:335–36. However, schoolbook authors did not have to attend college to be exposed to ideas concerning the effect of rhetoric on virtue. As William Chavat, Terence Martin, Henry May and David Lundberg have demonstrated, discussions of British rhetorical theory were widely available to American readers. See Chavat, chapter 3; Terence Martin, *The Instructed Vision: Scottish Common Sense Philosophy and the Origins of American Fiction* (Bloomington: Indiana Univ. Press, 1961), chapter 1; Henry May and David Lundberg, "The Enlightened Reader in America," *American Quarterly* 28 (1976), 262–71. *American Annals of* Education 1 (1832), 101; *The Floriad* 1 (1811), 33; Salma Hale, *History of the United States*, preface; "Eulogy of Washington, Delivered at the Request of the Legislature of Massachusetts, February 8, 1800, *Works of Fisher Ames,* ed. Seth Ames (Boston: Little, Brown and Company, 1854), 2:72.

146. Charles Stewart Davies, "An Address Delivered on the Commemoration at Fryeburg, Maine, May 19, 1825," quoted in Lawrence A. Cremin, *The American Common School: An Historic Conception* (New York: Teachers College, Columbia Univ., 1951), 31; Webster, *On the Education of Youth in America*, 65; Rush, *A Plan for the Establishment of Public Schools*, 14.; De Witt Clinton, *Speech of Governor Clinton to the Legislature of the State of New York, on the Sixth Day of January, 1819* (Albany, 1819), 9; "On Education," by "P. . . S. . . ," *West Carolina*, January 11, 1825, in Charles L. Coon, *The Beginnings of Public Education in North Carolina: A Documentary History 1790–1840* (Raleigh, NC: Publications of the North Carolina Historical Commission, 1908), 254.

147. For example, see Wood, *Radicalism of the American Revolution*, 148–55; John Locke, *Some Thoughts Concerning Education,* in *The Educational Writings of John Locke,* ed. James Axtell (Cambridge: Cambridge Univ. Press, 1968), 145; Axtell, introduction to *Some Thoughts Concerning Education,* 63–64.

148. John Locke, *An Essay Concerning Human Understanding* (1690; reprint, ed. Peter N. Nidditch, Oxford: Oxford Univ. Press, 1975), 104.

149. Locke, *Education,* 387–88.

150. Ibid., 171–72, 182.

151. Ibid., 122–23; ibid., 145. Locke's influence on child-rearing in the early national period, and Benjamin Rush's adoption of Lockean principles, are examined by Jacqueline S. Reinier, "Rearing the Republican Child: Attitudes and Practices in Post-Revolutionary Philadelphia," *William and Mary Quarterly* 39 (1982), 150–63.

152. Weems, *Life of George Washington,* 28–29.

153. Mason Locke Weems, *The Life of Gen. Francis Marion,* 4th ed. (Philadelphia: M. Carey, 1816), 54.

154. Ibid., 55.

155. Ibid., 68–69.

156. Ibid., 209.

157. Ibid., 210.

158. Ibid., 212–13.

159. Ibid., 213.

160. Fliegelman argues that expectations of voluntaristic marriage based on love and affection were created by Lockean pedagogy. See especially Fliegelman, *Prodigals and Pilgrims,* chapter 5. Weems, *Life of Gen. Francis Marion,* 205–7.

161. Grimshaw, *History of the United States,* 144.

162. Discussions of McCrea's significance in the iconography of the Revolution occur in Fliegelman, *Prodigals and Pilgrims,* 137–40; Kenneth Silverman, A *Cultural History of the Revolution,* 330–31; and Samuel Y. Edgerton, "The Murder of Jane McCrea: The Tragedy of an American Tableau d'Histoire," *Art Bulletin* 47 (1965), 481–92.

163. Humphreys, *Life of the Honorable Major-General Israel Putnam,* 67–70.

164. *The Analectic Magazine* 11 (1818), 254; Stipple by T. Kelly, for *The Columbian Magazine,* n. d. (Stauffer, *American Engravers Upon Copper and Steel,* no. 1629); Rush, *Plan for the Establishment of Public Schools,* 13–18.

165. See Wood, *Radicalism of the American Revolution,* 215–18; Waldstreicher, *In the Midst of Perpetual Fetes,* 74–77; John Patrick Diggins, *The Lost Soul of American Politics: Virtue, Self-Interest, and the Foundations of Liberalism* (New York: Basic Books, 1984), 20.

166. *Ohio Miscellaneous Museum* 1 (1822), 190–91.

167. Ferguson, "The American Enlightenment, 1750–1820," 535–36. See also Wood, *Radicalism of the American Revolution*, 359–60: "In a society of many scrambling, ordinary, and insignificant people, the power of genius and great-souled men no longer seemed to matter. . . . Greatness in America's colonial period may have been due almost entirely to the exertions of prominent individuals. But the American Revolution had created 'something of a general will'" that replaced the need for heroic individuals. Woodward, *The Columbian Plutarch,* introduction; Wilmer, "Observations on Reading," preface to *The American Nepos.*

168. Quoted in Fliegelman, *Prodigals and Pilgrims*, 104; Weems, *Life of George Washington*, 80–81.

169. My remarks about evangelicalism are based on the work of Rhys Isaac, Donald Mathews, and Dickson Bruce. See Isaac, *Transformation of Virginia*, chapters 8, 11, and 12; Donald G. Mathews, *Religion in the Old South* (Chicago: The Univ. of Chicago Press, 1977), especially chapter 2; and Dickson D. Bruce, Jr., *And They All Sang Hallelujah: Plain-Folk Camp-Meeting Religion, 1800–1845* (Knoxville: The Univ. of Tennessee Press, 1974), chapter 2. Mathews, ibid., 47.

170. Barbara Miller Solomon, introduction to *Travels in New England and New York*, by Timothy Dwight (1821–22; reprint, ed. Barbara Miller Solomon, Cambridge, MA: Harvard Univ. Press, 1969), 1:xxix, xxx, xxxiv; Vincent Freimarck, "Timothy Dwight's Brief Lives in *Travels in New England and New York,*" *Early American Literature* 8 (1973), 44–58; Shaffer, introduction to *History of Virginia,* by Edmund Randolph, xxiii–xxvi; Elson, *Guardians of Tradition*, 7; Joseph J. Ellis, *After the Revolution: Profiles of Early American Culture* (New York: W. W. Norton & Company, 1979), 35–37; Gilmore, *Reading Becomes a Necessity of Life*, 37. James M. Banner, Jr. provides an excellent discussion of the ideology of New England Federalists in chapter 1 of *To the Hartford Convention: The Federalists and the Origins of Party Politics in Massachusetts, 1789–1815* (New York: Alfred A. Knopf, 1970).

171. The decentralization of printing was part of a broader penetration of commercial activities into rural New England. William J. Gilmore discusses these developments in *Reading Becomes a Necessity of Life*, 352–61.

172. "'Home and School Life as They Were': Reminiscences of Benjamin Silliman, L. L. D.," *American Journal of Education* 26 (1876), 228; See David Hall, "Uses of Literacy in New England," 22–23. Education in rural New England began in the home with instruction in spelling and reading, and continued with summer and winter school classes established by local school districts. See Gilmore, *Reading Becomes a Necessity of Life*, 121–27. Nancy F.

Cott, *The Bonds of Womanhood: "Woman's Sphere" in New England, 1780–1835* (New Haven: Yale Univ. Press, 1977), 30–35. Carl N. Degler observes that women may have been the "sole formal educator" of children through age nine. See *At Odds: Women and the Family in America from the Revolution to the Present* (New York: Oxford Univ. Press, 1980), 74. See also Kathryn Kish Slar, "The Schooling of Girls and Changing Community Values in Massachusetts Towns, 1750–1820," *History of Education Quarterly* 33 (1993), 538–39.

173. Cott, *Bonds of Womanhood*, 95. Women's role as moral guardians is also examined by Mary Beth Norton, *Liberty's Daughters: The Revolutionary Experience of American Women, 1750–1800* (Boston: Little, Brown and Company, 1980), 24–50; Ruth H. Bloch, "American Feminine Ideals in Transition: The Rise of the Moral Mother, 1785–1815," *Feminist Studies* 4 (1978), 101–26; and Carl F. Kaestle, *Pillars of the Republic: Common Schools and American Society, 1780–1860* (New York: Hill and Wang, 1983), 26–27. Quoted in Cott, *Bonds of Womanhood*, 85; quoted in Linda K. Kerber, "Daughters of Columbia: Educating Women for the Republic, 1787–1805," in *Toward an Intellectual History of Women: Essays by Linda K. Kerber* (Chapel Hill: Univ. of North Carolina Press, 1997), 39; Norton, *Liberty's Daughters*, 248; Nina Baym, *American Women Writers and the Work of History, 1790–1860* (New Brunswick, NJ: Rutgers Univ. Press, 1995), 12. On the political implications of this role, see Linda K. Kerber, *Women of the Republic: Intellect and Ideology in Revolutionary America* (Chapel Hill: Univ. of North Carolina Press, 1980), 199–200, and Shirley Samuels, "The Family, the State, and the Novel in the Early Republic." *American Quarterly* 38 (1986), 381–95. J. Merton England and Norton Garfinkle offer two other views of the persistence of classical virtues in early nineteenth-century schoolbooks. England believes schoolbooks that stressed classical virtues were "the props of the state," for the country "could not endure" without the adoption of those values. Furthermore, he sees textbook lessons in classical virtue as a product of federalists who "wrung their hands over the passing of antique values ("The Democratic Faith in American Schoolbooks of the Republic, 1783–1861," *American Quarterly* 15 (1963), 191–99). Garfinkle argues that classical virtues such as benevolent disinterestedness and industry were taught so that the young would "accept without dissatisfaction the station which had fallen to their lot." ("Conservatism in American Textbooks, 1800–1860," *New York History* 35 (1954), 49–63).

174. Michael T. Gilmore's observations on the corporate view of narrative in the early republic helped me clarify my argument about the persistence of traditional forms of biography. See his "The Literature of the Revolutionary

and Early National Periods," 544–45. Weems, *Life of George Washington*, 4. Waldstreicher discusses the problem of differentiating real versus false displays of virtue in public celebrations (*In the Midst of Perpetual Fetes*, 64–65). Larzer Ziff, *Writing in the New Nation: Prose, Print, and Politics in the Early United States* (New Haven: Yale Univ. Press, 1991), and Mark R. Patterson, *Authority, Autonomy, and Representation in American Literature, 1776–1865* (Princeton: Princeton Univ. Press, 1988), provide insightful discussions of the problem as it occurs in early American novels.

175. *The American Museum* 5 (1789), 452.

176. *Lancaster Hive* 1 (1803), 76.

177. Weems, *Life of Gen. Francis Marion*, 106; ibid., 74.

178. Ibid., 239ff.

179. Ibid., 155–56.

180. Ibid., 156.

181. Ibid., 198–99. For other examples of Marion's propensity to talk about virtue, see the exchange with DeKalb on happiness and religion that constitutes most of chapter 11, and Marion's speech on the evils of drinking and gambling, 239ff.

182. Weems, *Life of Gen. Francis Marion*, 232.

183. Ibid., 169–70.

184. Ibid., 174–75.

185. Ibid., 131.

186. Ibid., 227.

187. Ibid., 241.

188. Weems to Horry, December 13, 1809, 2:427. For the growing American passion for romance fiction see Brown, Part I, and Robert B. Winans, "The Growth of a Novel-Reading Public in Late Eighteenth-Century America," *Early American Literature* 9 (1975), 267–75. Weems reported to Carey that *Charlotte Temple* was selling well, and in one letter lists small sales of *Ormond* and *Wieland* (Weems to Carey, March 24, 1801, 2:182–83). However, in their analysis of Virginia book inventories, Kett and McClung found surprisingly few novels. They explain their finding by suggesting that Virginians may have not been able to obtain the fiction they wanted to read. Moreover, readers may have been reluctant to buy novels, because reading them was perceived as a vice by many. Even so, Kett and McClung note, "there *was* a gradual growth of interest in fiction evidenced by estates inventories after 1800 and especially after 1810" (Kett and McClung, "Book Culture in Post-Revolutionary Virginia,"125–26). Jack Larkin notes that novels were not part of the inventory of the Merriam brothers, printers in Brookfield, Massachusetts, because

"reading of fiction . . . into the 1830s seems to have played a very limited role" in rural New England (Larkin, "The Merriams of Brookfield," 66). Philip Gura finds no novels whatsoever in the inventory of printer John Howe (Gura, "Early Nineteenth-Century Printing in Rural Massachusetts," 114–39). See chapter 1, "The Book in the New Republic," in Davidson, *Revolution and the Word,* for an extensive discussion about the rise of the novel, and issues printers had bringing novels to the public. Like his *Life of Washington,* Weems' biography of Marion departed from the norm of biographical writing too much to be accepted by other biographers and publishers. For example, William Allen and John Kingston used Peter Horry's version of Marion, not Weems', in their biographical dictionaries.

189. Weems, *Life of Gen. Francis Marion,* 9, 10, 13–14.

190. Ibid., 5. More of the same occurs on 256–57.

191. Ibid., 63.

192. Weems, *Life of George Washington,* 78–79.

193. *Practical Reading Lessons,* 133–34, 196, 225; [Anna C. Reed], *The Life of George Washington. Written for the American Sunday-School Union* (Philadelphia: American Sunday-School Union, 1829), 17, 265; [Samuel G. Goodrich], *The Life of George Washington* (Philadelphia: Collins and Hammay, 1832). Richard Slotkin examines the emergence of Boone as a hero in *Regeneration Through Violence: The Mythology of the American Frontier, 1600–1860* (Middletown, CT: Wesleyan Univ. Press, 1973), especially chapters 11 and 12. On Jackson as a hero, see John William Ward, *Andrew Jackson: Symbol For an Age* (New York: Oxford Univ. Press, 1955).

Illustrations

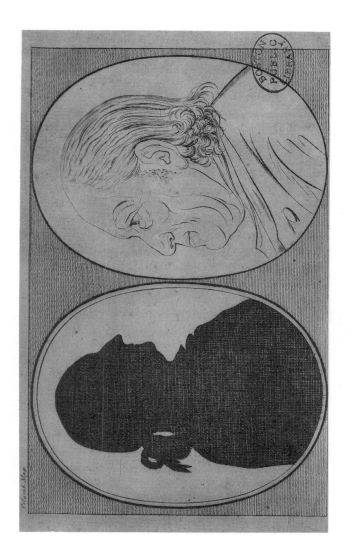

Figure 1: George Washington, *The Columbian Magazine*, 1788 (By courtesy of the Trustees of the Boston Public Library)

Figure 2: George Washington, *The Massachusetts Magazine*, 1791 (By permission of the Houghton Library, Harvard University)

GEORGE WASHINGTON ESQ.ᴿ

Philadᵃ Published for Thoˢ Condie Bookseller.

Figure 3: George Washington Esqʳ., *The Philadelphia Monthly Magazine, or Universal Repository*, 1798 (Rare Books Division, The New York Public Library, Astor, Lenos, and Tilden Foundations)

Figure 4: George Washington, *The Boston Magazine*, 1784 (By permission of the Massachusetts Historical Society)

GEN.WASHINGTON takes Command of the
American Army at Cambridge July 3d 1775.

Tisdale Sc.

GEN^L. WASHINGTON.

Engrav'd for C.Smith N-YORK.

Figure 5: Genl. Washington, *The Monthly Military Repository*, 1796 (Rare Books
Division, The New York Public Library, Astor, Lenos, and Tilden Foundations)

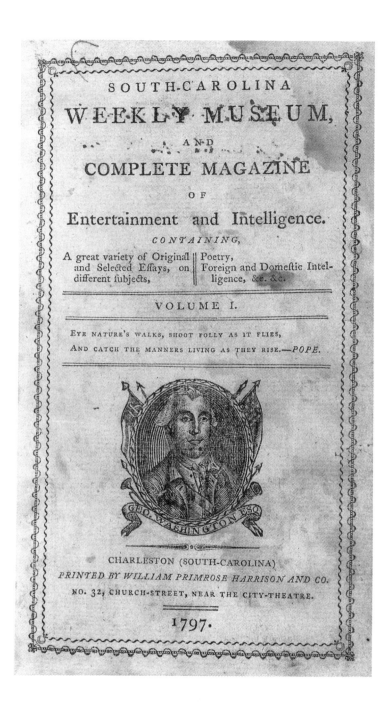

SOUTH-CAROLINA

WEEKLY MUSEUM,

AND

COMPLETE MAGAZINE

OF

Entertainment and Intelligence.

CONTAINING,

A great variety of Original || Poetry,
and Selected Essays, on || Foreign and Domestic Intel-
different subjects, || ligence, &c. &c.

VOLUME I.

EYE NATURE'S WALKS, SHOOT FOLLY AS IT FLIES,
AND CATCH THE MANNERS LIVING AS THEY RISE.——*POPE.*

GEO. WASHINGTON ESQ.

CHARLESTON (SOUTH-CAROLINA)
PRINTED BY WILLIAM PRIMROSE HARRISON AND CO.
NO. 32, CHURCH-STREET, NEAR THE CITY-THEATRE.

1797.

Figure 6: George Washington, *The South Carolina Weekly Museum*, 1797 (By courtesy of Clements Library, University of Michigan)

Barrelet Invt & Direxit   Lawson sculp

GENERAL WASHINGTON'S

RESIGNATION.

Published by B.Davies Philadᵃ 1ˢᵗ Febʸ 1799.

Figure 7: General Washington's Resignation, *The Philadelphia Magazine and Review*, 1799 (Boston Athenaeum)

Figure 8: Britannia, George Richardson, *Iconology*, 1779

Figure 9: Patriotism, George Richardson, *Iconology*, 1779

Figure 10: George Washington, *The New York Mirror*, 1831 (The Harvard Theatre Collection, The Houghton Library, Fredric Woodbridge Wilson, Curator)

Figure 11: Major General Warren, *The Boston Magazine*, 1784 (By permission of the Massachusetts Historical Society)

Figure 12: Maj.ʳ. Gen.ˡ. Greene, *The Columbian Magazine*, 1786 (By courtesy of the Trustees of the Boston Public Library)

Figure 13: Gen. Wayne, *The Polyanthos*, 1806 (By courtesy of the Trustees of the Boston Public Library)

Figure 14: Nicholas Biddle, *The Port Folio*, 1809 (Harvard College Library)

Edwin sc.

Figure 15: Anthony Wayne, *The Port Folio*, 1809 (Harvard College Library)

Figure 16: Daniel Morgan, *The Port Folio*, 1812 (Harvard College Library)

Figure 17: Henry Knox, *The Port Folio*, 1811 (Harvard College Library)

Figure 18: George Washington, Mason Locke Weems, *The Life and Memorable Actions of George Washington*, 1800 (Courtesy, American Antiquarian Society)

G. WASHINGTON.

Figure 19: George Washington, Mason Locke Weems, *A History, of the Life and Death, Virtues, and Exploits, of General George Washington* . . . , 2nd ed., 1800 (Courtesy, American Antiquarian Society)

Figure 20: George Washington, Mason Locke Weems, *A History, of the Life and Death, Virtues, and Exploits, of General George Washington* . . . , 3rd ed., 1800 (By permission of the Houghton Library, Harvard University)

Frontispiece

Death of Genl Montgomery

Figure 21: Death of Genl Montgomery, Mason Locke Weems, *The Life of George Washington; With Curious Anecdotes, Equally Honorable to Himself, and Exemplary to his Young Countrymen*, 8th ed., 1809 (Courtesy, American Antiquarian Society)

Page 77

Battle of Bunker's Hill & Death of Gen. Warren

Figure 22: Battle of Bunker's Hill & Death of Gen. Warren, Mason Locke Weems, *The Life of George Washington; With Curious Anecdotes, Equally Honorable to Himself, and Exemplary to his Young Countrymen*, 8th ed., 1809 (Courtesy, American Antiquarian Society)

To M. Iohn Gostlinge.

Loe Sisyphvs, that roles the reſtleſſe ſtone
To toppe of hill, with endleſſe toile, and paine:
Which beinge there, it tumbleth doune alone,
And then, the wretche muſt force it vp againe:
    And as it falles, he makes it ſtill aſcende;
    And yet, no toile can bringe this worke to ende.

This Sisyphvs: preſenteth Adams race.
The reſtleſſe ſtone: their trauaile, and their toile:
The hill, dothe ſhewe the daye, and eeke the ſpace,
Wherein they ſtill doe labour, worke, and moile.
    And thoughe till nighte they ſtriue the hill to clime,
    Yet vp againe, the morning nexte betime.

Vita humana propriè vti ferrum eſt: Ferrum ſi exerceas, conteritur: ſi non exerceas, tamen rubigo interficit. Item homines exercendo videmus conteri. Si
nihil exerceas, inertia atque torpedo plus detrimenti facit, quàm exercitatio.

Ouid. Metam. lib. 4.

Plat. de proſper.
Hanc rationem deus
ſequitur in bonis vi-
ris, quàm in diſcipu-
lis ſuis præceptores:
qui plus laboris ab
his exigunt, in qui-
bus certior ſpes eſt.

Aul. Gell. lib. 11. 14. 2.

Qui

Figure 23: Sisyphus, Geffery Whitney, *A Choice of Emblems.* Ed. Henry Greene, 1586; reprint, 1866.

G. WASHINGTON.

Love righteousness, ye that be judges of
the earth : think of the Lord with a good
heart, and in simplicity of heart seek him.

Figure 24: G. Washington, *The New England Primer, Much Improved*, 1796 (Rare Book
Department, Free Library of Philadelphia)

His Excellency GEN. WASHINGTON,
Prefident of the United States.

" Great without pomp, without ambition brave,
" Proud not to conquer fellow-men, but fave.

Figure 25: His Excellency Gen. Washington, President of the United States, *The History of America Abridged for the Use of Children*, 1795 (Rare Book Department, Free Library of Philadelphia)

and putting the torch to the wolf's nofe, found fhe
was dead. Then taking her by the ears, he kicked
the rope, and his friends drew him and the wolf out
together.

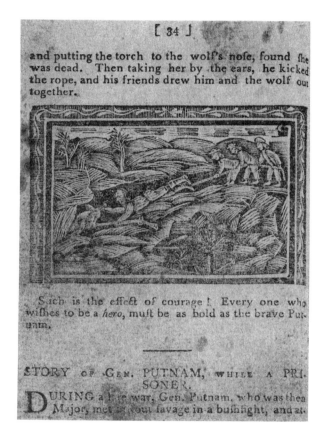

Such is the effect of courage! Every one who
wifhes to be a *hero*, muft be as bold as the brave Putnam.

STORY of GEN. PUTNAM, WHILE A PRI-
SONER.

DURING a late war, Gen. Putnam, who was then
Major, met a ftout favage in a bufhfight, and at.

Figure 26: Israel Putnam and the Wolf, Noah Webster, *Little Reader's Assistant*, 1790
(Rare Books Division, The New York Public Library, Astor, Lenos, and Tilden
Foundations)

with the butt ends of their muskets, and then reluctantly retreated.

11. In this battle, 1054 of the British were killed and wounded; of the Americans, 453. The British officers were astonished at the result : they had despised the Americans before, and never imagined that a collection of people, who had not learnt the art of war, commanded by no experienced officers, and but poorly provided with arms and ammunition, could make such havoc among disciplined troops.

12. This battle, though it was fought on Breed's Hill, is called the battle of Bunker Hill. The Americans were driven back, indeed ; but this happened only because their ammunition was expended. It gave the people great courage, for it showed that they could beat the British Regulars in a fair fight.

13. Yet the Americans, though they rejoiced at their partial success, had much occasion for sorrow. Many of their friends and neighbors had been killed, and among these was Gen. Warren, who was greatly beloved by all the people. He was fighting in the midst of the battle, when a British officer, who knew him, took a gun from a soldier, and shot him through the head.

Death of General Warren.

the battle. 11. Loss of the British ? Of the Americans ? British officers ? 12. Where was the battle

CHAP. LIV.

REVOLUTION.—CONTINUED.

1. The people of the colonies, finding it necessary to have some general government, had sent some of their wisest men to Philadelphia, to manage public affairs. These were called the Continental Congress. They appointed George Washington of Virginia, Commander in Chief of the American Armies, and in about a fortnight after the battle of Bunker Hill, he reached Cambridge, three miles from Boston. He found about 14,000 militia in the neighborhood, and immediately began to exert himself to teach them the art of war.

2. I shall not be able to tell you of all the interesting events that occurred during the Revolution. The story of them would fill a large book. I shall only give you a few details, and leave you to read the whole history in some larger work. The war soon spread over the country, and many skirmishes took place between the provincials, and the British soldiers.

3. During the latter part of the year 1775, two expeditions were sent against Canada ; one, consisting of 3000 men, was put under the command of Gen. Schuyler, and went by the way of Lake Champlain ; the other, consisting of 1100 men, and commanded by Gen. Arnold, went up the Kennebec river, and crossed the wilderness to Quebec.

4. The soldiers, under the command of Arnold, suffered incredible hardships. For several days, they were almost en-

of Bunker Hill fought ? Why were the Americans driven back ? Why did the battle of Bunker Hill encourage the Americans ? 13. Gen. Warren ? Describe the picture.
1. Continental Congress ? Washington ? Militia ? 2. What of the war ? 3. General Schuyler ? Gen. Arnold ? 4. What of his ex-

Figure 27: Death of General Warren, [Samuel Griswold Goodrich], *The First Book of History, for Children and Youth*, 1831 (Harvard College Library)

Figure 28: Israel Putnam and the Wolf, *Juvenile Miscellany*, 1827 (By permission of the Houghton Library, Harvard University)

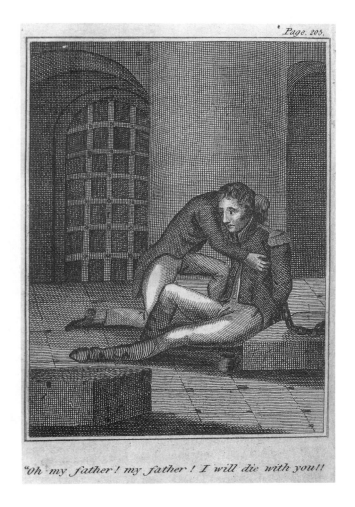

"Oh my father! my father! I will die with you!!

Figure 29: Oh my father! my father! I will die with you!!, Mason Locke Weems, *The Life of Gen. Francis Marion*, 7th ed., 1821 (Rare Books Division, The New York Public Library, Astor, Lenos, and Tilden Foundations)

J.Broughan.

T.Kelley.

Genl Warren taking leave of his wife and child
on the eve of the battle of Bunker Hill.

W.L.Ormsby, Printer

Desired & Engraved Expressly for the Columbian Magazine.

Figure 30: Genl. Warren taking leave of his wife and child on the eve of the battle of Bunker Hill, *The Columbian Magazine*, n.d.   (Boston Athenaeum)

Index

Abbott, J.S.C. 93
Academic Speaker (John Walker)
    48
Adams, Hannah 65
Adams, John 10
Adams, Rufus 61
Addison, Joseph 75–76
"Advice to a Young Tradesman"
    (Benjamin Franklin) 51
Affection. *See also* Friendship
    filial 26, 49–50, 82–86, 90
    marital 86–89
    social harmony, as ideal 6, 27,
        89–90, 91–92
Alexandria, Va. 14, 15, 16
Allen, William 4
Altar (emblem) 35
*American Biographical and
    Historical Dictionary*
    (William Allen) 4
American Geography (Jedediah
    Morse) 3, 31, 45, 61
American Journal of Education 93
American Museum (magazine) 30,
    95
American Nepos (John Wilmer) 56
American Preceptor (Caleb
    Bingham) 45–46, 47, 48, 51

American Sunday School Union
    105
American Universal Magazine 34
Ames, Fisher 80
Analectic Magazine 88
Ancestor images, use in ancient
    Rome 8
Andre, Maj. John 4, 63–64
Anecdotes. *See also individual
    heroes' names*
    dangers of, for children 74–75
    emergence of, in biography 29–
        30, 71–72
    in *History of the Life of
        Washington* 6, 15–17, 55–56
    in *Life,* revised 19–21, 27, 94–
        95
    re minor heroes 38, 99–102
    and realism 95–99, 104
    public *vs.* private 5, 16, 20–22,
        95
    use of, in schoolbooks 47, 61
Arnold, Benedict 64
Art of Speaking (James Burgh) 48
Artes Historicae 7
Arts
    emblems for 36–37
    and rhetoric 48

Avarice, vs. virtue 72

Baker, W.S. 4
Bancroft, Aaron 3, 6, 7
Barralet, John James 35–36
Bartlett, Montgomery 66–67
Battle of Bunker Hill (John
    Trumbull) 60
Battles
    Braddock 57–58
Bunker Hill 38, 58, 67, 68, 88
    Charleston 85
    Cowpens 67
    Fort Necessity 13
    Lodi 57
    Monmouth 95
    Monongahela 14
    Quebec 58, 68
    Sullivan's Island 84
    Ticonderoga 39
Beattie, James 25
Bell, John 31–32, 33–34
Benevolence (virtue) 28, 48–49,
    61, 94
Bible 10, 20
Bibliotheca Washingtoniana 4
Biddle Nicholas 41, 92
Bingham, Caleb 45–46, 47, 48, 51,
    61
*Biographical Memoirs of the
    Illustrious Gen. George
    Washington* (Thomas
    Condie) 4
*Biographical Sketches of Great
    and Good Men* (Lydia Child)
    61
Biographies, of American
    Revolutionary heroes. *See
    also individual heroes' and
    authors' names*

civic use of *xiii-xiv*, 71–72, 92,
    94
commercial success of 5–6, 31
conventional style of 5, 6–10,
    14–15, 94–95
early 3–5
exemplary. *See* Example(s)
falsehoods in 16, 57, 73–74
graphic portraits with 30–31,
    57–58
as history 7
Johnsonian concept of 10, 21,
    22
market for, southern 6, 10–13
of minor heroes 38–43
need for 12–13, 22
public *vs.* private experience in
    5,16, 20–22
realism in 95–105
as source for schoolbooks 45,
    47, 51, 61–69, 94
*Biography of Principle Military
    and Naval Heroes
    Comprehending Details of
    Their Achievements during
    the Revolutionary and Late
    Wars* (Thomas Wilson) 5, 71
Bioren, John 57
Blackwood's Magazine 30
Blair, Hugh 50, 79
Bolingbroke, Viscount Henry
    Saint John 7–8
Book buyers
    New England 92–94
    patriotic 31
    southern 6, 10–13
Boston, Mass., publishing in 29
Boston Magazine 34, 37, 38
Braddock, Gen. Edward 14, 58
Britannia (emblem) 35–36
Brown, Charles Brockden 41

Buckingham, Joseph 93
Burgh, James 48
Burgoyne, Gen. John 41

Caldwell, Charles 4, 72
Calumet, Indian (emblem) 35, 36
Campaign of 1781 (Henry Lee) 40
Carey, Mathew
    American writings, use of 30–
        31
    bookstock choices 11–13
    Greene sketch by 38
    Lee anecdote by 95
    and schoolbook market 51–52
    and Weems
        re bookstores 10–13
        friendship expectations 27–28
        re Washington biography 56–
            57
Cato (Joseph Addison) 75–76, 89
Character. *See* Virtue(s)
Character sketches. *See*
    Biographies
Charless, Joseph 3
Child, Lydia Maria 61
Children. *See* Education
Cincinnatus 36, 66
Citizenship. *See* Education;
    Example(s); Patriotism
Clark, Jonathan 7, 24
Clarke, Edward Jr. 81
Climate, and virtue 53–54
Clinton, Gov. De Witt 80
Coercion, in education 81–82
Columbian Magazine 32, 38, 88
Columbian Plutarch (Thomas
    Woodward) 5
Columbian Preceptor (Nathaniel
    Heaton, Jr.) 71
Common School Manual
    (Montgomery Bartlett) 66–67

Competitiveness. *See* Rivalry
Condie, Thomas 4, 33
Confession, evangelical 91
Connecticut Magazine 34
Cooper, James Fenimore 99
Cornucopia (emblem) 35, 36
Cornwallis, Gen 85
Corry, John 3, 5
Courage (virtue) 36, 67–68, 90
Crevecoeur, J. Hector St. John de
    53–54
Cudjo
    overseer 99–100
    pilot 104

D'Estang, Ct. 103
Dance, in Virginia 17
Daveis, Charles Stewart 80
Death (virtue) 67–68, 75–76
*Death of General Montgomery in
    the Attack on Quebec* (John
    Trumbull) 58
"Death of General Warren" (illus.)
    60
*Death of General Warren at the
    Battle of Bunker's Hill* (John
    Trumbull) 58
*Delaplaine's Repository of the
    Lives and Portraits of
    Distinguished Americans* 4–
    5, 55
Dennie, Joseph
    political motives of 42–43, 92
    Washington portrait
        interpretation 37
    Washington sketches by 30
Dialect, use of by Weems 103–104
Dickinson, John 73
Dictionaries, biographical 4–5
Didacticism, and portraits 34–37,
    46–47, 58–59

Dionysus of Halicarnassus 8
Drinking, in Virginia 17
Drunkard's Looking Glass (Mason
    Locke Weems) 97
Dueling, southern 19, 54
Durand, Asher B. 36
Duty, filial (virtue) 49–50, 82–86,
    90
Dwight, Timothy 92

Eagle (emblem) 35, 36, 56
Education
    and citizenship *xiii-xiv*, 71–72,
        73–74, 80–81, 92, 94
    by example. *See* Example(s)
    by images. *See* Images
    in rhetoric 47–48, 51
    by schoolbooks. *See*
        Schoolbooks
    Washington's. *See* Washington,
        George
    by women 93–94
Edwin, David 41
Elements of Criticism (Henry
    Home) 78
Elocution. *See* Reading aloud
Emblems. *See also individual
    symbols*
    allegorical nature of 34–35, 36–
        37, 59
    definition 46
    didactic *vs.* ornamental 46–47,
        58–59
    knowledge of, by readers 37
    schoolbooks, use in 46, 58–61
    source of 35
    vitality of convention 59–61
Empathy (virtue). *See* Sympathy
Emulation, of virtues *vs.* faults 74–
    75
Equanimity. *See* Self-control

Essai sur la physiognomonie *(John
    Caspar Lavater)* 32
Essay on Human Understanding
    (John Locke) 81
Essay on Taste (Alexander
    Gerard) 77–78
*Essay on the Life of the Honorable
    Major-General Israel Putnam*
    (David Humphreys)
    anecdotes in 30, 87–88
    as history 7
    as source for magazines 38
Evangelism, as alternative to
    rivalry 91–92
Example(s)
    in biography 7–9
    vs. coercion 81–82
    dangers of 22, 74–75
    precedent for 7–8
    proponents of 7–10, 61–69, 71–
        74
    theories of
        American educational 79–82
        British psychological 75–79
    in Weems' biography of
        Washington 13–19, 82–83
    in Weems' revision 19–28, 94–
        95

Fame (emblem) 36
Father, as virtuous example 22–26,
    82–85, 88–89
Federalism. *See also* Patriotism
    heroic images created by 92
    in magazine sketches 42–43
    in schoolbooks 45
Feeling, capacity for. *See*
    Sympathy
Female figure (emblem) 35
Fidelity (virtue) 63–64

First Book of History (Samuel Goodrich) 60–61, 66
First Lessons in the History of the United States (Caroline Matilda Thayer) 68
Folwell, Samuel 36
Franklin, Benjamin 50, 51
Freeman, Douglas Southall 16
French and Indian War
Putnam's experiences in 30, 39
in Washington's biography 9
Washington's patriotism during 53
Washington's role in 13
Friendship. *See also* Affection
filial 82, 83, 90
in schoolbooks 50
in Weems' biographies 26–27, 91–92
Weems' own hopes for 27–28
Gambling, in Virginia 17–18
Gates, Horatio
biographical portrait of 4
medal in honor of 41
as virtuous example 92
Weems' criticism of 96
Gerard, Alexander 77–78
Goodrich, Samuel Griswold 60–61, 66, 105
Greene, Gen. Nathaniel
biographical sketches of 4, 5, 29, 38, 67
engraving of 38
life of, as history 7
Grimshaw, William 87

Hagiography, as precursor to biography 7
Hale, Capt. Nathan 65
Hale, Salma 80
Hall, Samuel Read 47

Harmony, social
vs. rivalry 6, 91–92
Washington and 17, 19, 26–27
Harris, Samuel 41
Hayne, Col. Isaac 40, 85–86
Helmet (emblem) 35, 36
Heroes, American Revolutionary.
See also individual names
affections of
for parents 83–86
for wives and children 87–89
falsehoods about 73–74
flawed, portrayal of 95–97
forgetting, danger of 72–73
illustrations of. *See* Illustrations
images of. *See* Images
in magazines 29–43
minor, in Weems' work 99–102
realism about, shift to 95–105
relationship to community 7, 20–21, 61–62
Hessians, Washington's treatment of 26–27
History (emblem) 37
History, exemplary. *See* Example(s)
History of South Carolina (David Ramsay) 54
History of the American Revolution (David Ramsay) 54
History of the Life and Death, Virtues and Exploits, of Gen. George Washington (Mason Locke Weems)
anecdotal emphasis of 6, 55–56, 82–83, 91–92, 94
criticism of, contemporary 30
illustrations in 56–57
price 6

revision of, 1808. *See Life of
    George Washington*
  structure 13–19, 94
  Weems' market analysis for 12–
    13
*History of the Rise, Progress and
  Termination of the American
  Revolution* (Mercy Otis
  Warren) 72
History of the United States
  (William Grimshaw) 87
History of Virginia (Edmund
  Randolph) 92
Home, Henry 78
Honesty (virtue), *vs.* avarice 72.
  See also Washington, George
Honor, southern 18–19
Horry, Peter 98, 102, 103
Horse racing, and southern rivalry
  17
Hospitality, southern 18
Houdon, Jean-Antoine 5
Hume, David 76–77
Humility (virtue) 14, 24–25, 53
Humphreys, David
  anecdotes about Putnam 30, 38,
    87–88
  sketch of Washington 3, 31, 45

Iconology (George Richardson)
  35,36
Ideas, as perceptions 76–77
Ignorance, threat to republic 80–
  81
Illustrations. *See also* Emblems;
    and individual heroes' names
  didactic 34–37
  in magazines 29, 30, 42–43, 88
  in schoolbooks 46, 56–61

Images. *See also* Anecdotes;
    Example(s); *and individual
    heroes' names*
  dangers of 74–75
  in magazines 29–31, 42–43, 92,
    95–96
  of minor heroes 99–102, 104–
    105
  power to stimulate virtues 8–9,
    71–82
  realistic 95–99, 104
  in schoolbooks 47, 51, 61–69
  of sentiment 89–90, 91–92
Indians (emblem) 37
Industry (virtue) 50–51, 54–55
*Introduction to the National
    Reader* (John Pierpont) 61
Isaac, Rhys 17

James, William Dobein 4, 7
Jasper, Sgt. 84, 99
Jefferson, Thomas 42, 52
Johnson, Samuel
  concept of biography 10, 21
  value of biography for 22
Johnson, William 4, 7
Jones, John Paul 4, 73
Juba, Numidian Prince 76
Juvenile Mentor (Albert Picket) 61
Juvenile Miscellany (John
    Putnam) 62

Keatinge, George 56
Kingston, John 4
Knickerbocker literary school 36
Knox, Henry
  profile of 4
  "System of Virtue" 50
  virtues of 41–42, 92

Lacedemodians, as respectors of
  elders 50
Lancaster Hive (magazine) 95
Language, abstract *vs.* particular
  77–79
Laurens, Henry 103
Lavater, John Caspar 32
Lawson, Alexander 34
*Lectures to School-Masters, on
  Teaching* (Samuel Read Hall)
  47
Lee, Charles 4, 30–31, 95–96, 104
Lee, Henry 40, 67
Lessons in Elocution (William
  Scott) 46, 47, 48–49, 50–51
Letters from an American Farmer
  (Crevecoeur) 54
"Letters on the Study and Use of
  History" (Bolingbroke) 8, 9
Life of Gen. Francis Marion
  (Mason Locke Weems) *xiv*, 4,
  40
  filial affection portrayed in 84
  form of 102–104
  realism in 96–99
*Life of George Washington; With
  Curious Anecdotes, Equally
  Honorable to Himself, and
  Exemplary to his Young
  Countrymen* (Mason Locke
  Weems)
  anecdotes in 19–20, 22–27, 94–
  95
  innovation in 20–21, 22
  as reflection of Weems' hopes
  27–28
  as schoolbook 46, 51–56
Life of John Paul Jones (John
  Henry Sherburne) 7
Literary Casket (magazine) 34

Literary Miscellany (magazine) of
  Cambridge, Mass. 32, 33
Literary Miscellany (magazine) of
  New York 33
Little Reader's Assistant (Noah
  Webster) 45, 60
Lives (Plutarch) 7
Locke, John 81–82, 83
Lord Kames. *See* Home, Henry
Love. *See* Affection; Friendship;
  Sympathy

M'Crea, Jane 86–87
M'Queen, Alexander 96
Madison, James 9
Magazines
  biographies as sources for 29–
  31
  heroes in 31–43
  illustrations in 29, 30, 42–43, 88
  images in 29–31, 42–43, 92,
  95–96
  publishing centers for 29
  readership of 43, 116
Male figure (emblem) 36
Marion, Gabriel 102–103
Marion, Gen. Francis
  anecdotes about
    drinking 96–97
    love of liberty 89
    relationship with soldiers 97–
    99
  biography, success of 4
  in magazines 40
Marshall, Elihu, 55
Marshall, John 3, 6, 29; view of
  biography as history 7, 9–10
Massachusetts Magazine 31, 33,
  74
Mayo, Col. 19

Memories of Nathaniel Greene
(Charles Caldwell) 72
Memorization, aided by emblems
59
Mercer, Gen. Hugh 57
Merriams (printers) 45
Minerva (emblem) 36
Modesty. *See* Humility
Montesquieu 34, 38, 53
Montgomery, Richard 68
Monthly Anthology (magazine) 30
Monthly Military Repository
(magazine) 34
Morality. *See* Virtue(s)
Morgan, Daniel 41, 67, 92
Morris, Robert 73
Morse, Jedediah 3, 31, 45
Mother at Home (J.S.C. Abbott)
93–94
Motte, Mrs. 101
Mt. Vernon, Va. 3, 35
Muckleworth, Maj. 100
Music (emblem) 36

Nadel, George 7
National Magazine 38
National School Manual (M.R.
Bartlett) 61
Nationalism. *See* Patriotism
Nationality, and virtue 64, 100
Necklace (emblem) 36
*New American Biographical
Dictionary* (John Kingston) 4
New Biographical Dictionary
(Thomas Rogers) 72
New England Primer *59–60*
New York Magazine 40
New York Mirror (magazine) 36
Niagara Falls (emblem) 37
Norman, John
Warren engraving by 38

Washington portrait by 34, 37

Oak-leaf garland (emblem) 37
*Observation on the Climate in
Different Parts of America*
(Hugh Williamson) 54
Ogilvie, John 79
Ohio Miscellaneous Museum
(magazine) 29, 40
Olive branch (emblem) 35
Oral culture, southern 6, 20
Oxen (emblem) 36

Painting (emblem) 36
Parenting. *See also* Affection,
filial
danger of using example 74–75
by example 8, 23–25, 69, 82–83
Locke's theory of 81–82
women's role in 93–94
Patriotism. *See also* Education;
Federalism; Republicanism
in American magazines 30–31
avarice *vs.* 72
and benevolence 48–50
book sales related to 12–13, 55
familial love *vs.* 88–89
and realism 95–105
and schoolbook authors 64–65
as vanity 31
Paulding, John 63, 64
Payne, Mr., dispute with
Washington 15–16, 19, 26
Peace (emblem) 35
Peale, Charles Willson 8, 34, 38
Penn, Mr. 19
Perceptions, Hume's theory of 76–
77
Philadelphia, publishing history 29
*Philadelphia Magazine and
Review* 34

Philadelphia Monthly Magazine, or Universal Repository (1798) 4, 33
Philadelphia Repertory (magazine) 36, 38
Picket, Albert 61
Pierpont, John 61
Piety (virtue) 52–53, 94, 105
Plan for the Establishment of Public Schools (Benjamin Rush) 80
Pleasing, art of (virtue) 50
Plow (emblem) 36
Plutarch 7
Polyanthos (magazine) 39, 41, 72
Pope, Alexander 76
Port Folio (magazine) 4, 29, 32
  biography of Schuyler 73
  circulation of 116
  interpretation of engraving in 37
  use of portraits in 30, 41–42
Portico (magazine) 55
Portraits. *See* Illustrations
Practical Reading Lessons on the Three Great Duties (1830) 63, 104–105
Priestley, Joseph 79
Profit, *vs.* classical virtues 90
Protestantism, evangelical 91
Publishing
  centers, post-Rev. 29
  and patriotism 31, 42–43, 64–65, 92
  of schoolbooks 45–46, 92–93
Putnam, Israel
  biography of 3
  vs. Cincinnatus 66
  emblematic illustration of 60
  imprisonment ordeal 87–88
  in magazines 30, 38–40
  sketch of 4
  war years 39–40
  and wolf 38–39, 46, 61–63

Quarter races, southern 17–18

Ramsay, David 3, 7, 54, 71, 72
Randolph, Edmund 92
Rationality, *vs.* sensation 75–79
Readers. *See* Schoolbooks
Reading aloud, teaching 47–48.
  See also Rhetoric; Schoolbooks
Realism, advent in biography 95–105
Reed, Anna 105
Repository of the Lives and Portraits of Distinguished Americans (Joseph Delaplaine) 55
Republicanism, and virtue 80–81.
  See also Patriotism
Respect for elders (virtue) 50
Rhetoric. *See also* Schoolbooks
  British theories about 75–79
  readings for practice of 48–51
  techniques for 48, 51
Richardson, George, emblem vocabulary of 35–36
Rickett's Circus, Philadelphia 34, 35
Rivalry, southern 5, 17–19
Rock (emblem) 37
Rogers, Maj. Robert 40
Rogers, Thomas 72
Rope (emblem) 62
Rush, Benjamin 68, 80, 88–89

Sabbath schools 45
Sacrifice (virtue) 62–69, 88–89
Saratoga, N.Y. 41

Schoolbooks. *See also* Rhetoric
  authors' sources 45
  demand for 45–46
  in early republic 47–51
  emblems in 46–47, 58–61
  heroes' anecdotes in 45
  length of passages in 51
  Life of Washington as 51–56
  reading aloud, teaching 47–48
  sales of 45
  structure, typical 46
  virtues promoted in 46, 47, 48–
    51
  Weems' plans for 46, 51–56
Schools, New England 45
Schuyler, Philip 4, 42, 73, 92
Scott, William 46, 47
Scottish Enlightenment ideas 75,
    89
Self-control (virtue), and
    industrialization 94
Sherburne, John Henry 4, 73
Silliman, Benjamin 93
Sincerity (virtue) 50
Sisyphus (emblem) 58–59
*Sketch of the Life of Brig. Gen.
  Francis Marion* (William
    Dobein James) 4, 7
Sloth, *vs.* industry 55
Smith, Samuel Stanhope 9
South Carolina Weekly Museum
    (magazine) 34
Southern Review (magazine) 40
*Spelling Book of the English
  Language* (Elihu Marshall)
    55
Spirit of the Laws (Montesquieu)
    53
Spy (James Fenimore Cooper) 99
Stoicism (virtue), shift away from
    89–90

Stoney Point, N.Y. 67
Stork (emblem) 49
Storytelling, southern 6, 20
Stuart, Gilbert 57
Sully, Thomas 60
Sword (emblem) 35, 36
Symbolism, allegorical. *See*
    Emblems
Sympathy (virtue)
  evoking, theories of 75–79
  in heroes 5, 14–15, 39–40
  in reading aloud 47–48
  and social harmony 27
  "System of Virtue," Henry Knox
    50

Tanner, Benjamin 57
Temple of Fame (emblem) 35
Thayer, Caroline Matilda 68
Theater, and virtue 75–76
Thomas, Isaiah 31
Thoughts Concerning Education
    (John Locke) 81
Tisdale, Elkanah 34
Tocqueville, Alexis de 31
Travels in New England and New
    York *(Timothy Dwight)* 92
Treatise of Human Nature (David
    Hume) 76–77
Treaty of Paris (1783) 3
Trenchard, James 38
Trumbull, John 57, 60
Trumpet (emblem) 36

Vanwert, Isaac 63, 64
Villiers, Count de 13
Violence, in Virginia 6, 18, 19
Virginia
  book market 10–11
  climate, influence on virtue 54
  dances 17

illiteracy 20
rivalry 17–19
social relations 6
storytelling in 20
violence in 6, 18, 19
Virtue(s). *See also individual*
virtues and individual heroes'
names
classical republican *xii*
examples of. *See* Example(s)
public *vs.* private 10, 16, 20–22,
94–95
relevance, after Revolution 72
schoolbook promotion of 46,
47, 48–51
shift in, away from classical 89–
91, 104–105
and social status 62–63
and survival of republic 68–69,
71, 73–74, 80–81, 92
teaching. *See* Education;
Example(s)
Visual images. *See* Illustrations

Waldo, Albigence 30
Walker, John 48
Warren, Joseph
biographical sketches of 4, 5
death of 67
Norman engraving of 38
virtues of 88–89
Warren, Mercy Otis 72
Washington, George
affection, filial 26, 83
anecdotes about
ale cakes 66, 95–96
apple-sharing 22–23
ball, attending 17
cabbage seeds 25, 82, 83
cherry tree 19, 23–24, 25, 26,
66, 82–83

disputes, resolving 26–27
education of 22–26, 82–83
friendship 26–27
and Gen. Braddock 14
illustrations of 57–58
and Mr. Payne 15–16, 19, 26,
66
and Mr. Potts 52–53
praying 52–53, 105
public *vs.* private 5, 16, 20–
22, 95
sympathy for poor 15
benevolence 53
biographies of 3–6, 9–10, 13–
28, 30, 31–37, 51–56, 71, 92,
94–95, 105
cult of 3
disinterestedness 5
education of, by example 22–
26, 82–83
father of 22–26, 83
French and Indian War 13, 53
honesty 23–25, 53, 66, 83
humility 14, 24–25, 53
industry 53–54, 55
magazine coverage of 31–37
modesty 14
passions, control of 14, 15–16,
26–27
patriotism 53, 83
physical traits, and character 9,
31–32
piety 52–53
portraits of
in dictionary 5
didactic 34–37
popular 33
in schoolbooks 59–60
use of, by Weems 46, 56–58
veracity of 57, 113
presidency years 9

self-control 15–17, 19
sympathy 5, 14–15, 27
*Washington's Passage into the
    Delaware* (Thomas Sully) 60
Washington's Political Legacies 4,
    5
Wayne, Anthony
    biographical sketches of 4, 5
    courage of 67
    in magazines 40–41, 92
Wayne, C.P 3, 10
Wealth, threat to virtue 72
Webster, Noah 45, 46, 56, 60
Weekly Register 72
Weems, Mason Locke
    anecdotes, use of 15–17, 19–22,
        27–28, 82–86, 94–95
    and Beattie anecdote 25
    biography of Marion 96–104
    biography of Washington. *See
        History of the Life...*
    biography of Washington, rev.
        *See Life of George
        Washington*
    book market analysis 6, 10–13,
        46, 51–52
    on book prices 108
    bookstore idea 10–11
    and Carey. *See* Carey, Mathew
    dialect, use of 103–104
    fictional details, use of 16
    as homilist 98–102
    industry, belief in 54
    and Johnsonian biography 21–
        22
    and Marshall's biography of
        Washington 10
    minor heroes, focus on 99–102
    portraits, use of 46–47, 56–57
    realism, shift to 96–99
    as romance writer 102–103

and schoolbook market 46, 51–
    56
society as portrayed by 91–92
tales of sentiment, use of 89–90,
    91
virtues, view of *xiii-xiv*, 21–22,
    71
Wemyss, Maj. 100–101
Whear, Degory 7
Whitney, Geffery 58–59
Wick, Wendy 35
Williams, David 63, 64
Williams, John M. 4, 5
Williamson, Hugh 54
Wilmer, James Jones 90
Wilmer, John 56, 61
Wilson, Thomas 5, 71
Women
    anti-British 101–102
    as moral guardians 93–94
Woodward, Thomas 5
Wright, Joseph 33, 34
Wyandot Indians 87
Wyatt-Brown, Bertram 18

Yarmouth (frigate) 41
Yarnall, Peter 86
*Young Gentleman and Lady's
    Explanatory Monitor* (Rufus
    Adams) 61